CW01572812

We Sing a Song of Sadness

Former political prisoners in Tibet speak out

With poems and recollections by the late Ngodup Paljor

Written by: Billy Jackson
Edited by: Sarah Jackson, Lobsang Sangay, Tyler DeWaal

PublishAmerica
Baltimore

ISBN: 1-4137-1677-6
PUBLISHED BY PUBLISHAMERICA, LLLP
www.publishamerica.com
Baltimore

Printed in the United States of America

Foreword

by Tenzin Choegyal, brother of the Dalai Lama

The last fifty years of history on the roof of the world is written in Tibetan blood by the pens of modern Chinese emperors and their court.

Choegyal

June 28, 1999

Tenzin Choegyal
Brother of His Holiness the Dalai Lama
28 June, 1999

Acknowledgements

The following individuals and organizations must be recognized for their kind help and support, without which this book would not exist.

Rinchen Khando Choegyal and her husband, Rinpoche Tenzin Choegyal, Rapten and Khando Chazotsang, the International Committee of Lawyers for Tibet, the Women's Commission for Refugee Women and Children, the Tibetan Center for Human Rights and Democracy, Denise Lassaw, W. King Jackson, the Japanese communist in Paris, Kalsang Phuntsok, the Tibetan Government-In-Exile, especially the Department of Health, the Gu-Chu-Sum Ex-Political Prisoners Association, and a monk in Tibet who helped us when it might have been in his self-interest not to.

Introduction

When the Chinese ambassador to the United States visited Utah and made appearances at Brigham Young University and Utah Valley State College, a student asked him about human rights in Tibet during an open-question period. The ambassador suggested that the curious student "go and visit Tibet" for herself. He assured all in attendance that the Tibetans were doing better than ever. He defined this as higher GDP in the region and longer life expectancy.

Later, I got the chance to speak with him myself. We had a long discussion in which he sleekly maneuvered around every one of my questions, finally promising me that human rights violations claims were "lies," again quoting memorized GDP and life expectancy statistics to support his claim. I wondered what GDP and life expectancy had to do with human rights. Before we left, he extended the same challenge to me that he had earlier to the BYU student: "go and see for yourself." Though the Tibetan refugee friends who were with me could never return while the present government remained ruler of their country, I could. Two months later I was on a plane from Kathmandu to Lhasa.

My sojourn in Tibet left me breathless with memories of an amazing land tucked away on the roof of the world. For eleven days I was audience to fantastic peaks, a wonderfully friendly people, and a breathtaking history for all to see in the form of hillside forts and monasteries that dot a landscape more vast, more bleak, and more beautiful than any I'd ever seen. Sadly, the saga of the Tibetan nation has ceased to be written by any Tibetan, but rather may be testified by the brothels, discos, and ugly tile and tin buildings that have overgrown the small Tibetan neighborhoods. The Chinese government's policy of population transfer has made the Tibetans a minority in many parts of their own land. The "institutions" that have resulted from this mass migration attest to the type of influence that the PRC policy has had on the Land of the Snows. Visiting Tibet and seeing it with my own eyes was enough to invigorate my passion to fight for the rights—and the simple human dignity—that the Tibetans deserve as people. Visiting Dharamsala afterwards, however—and speaking to ex-political prisoners and exile-government officials—was more eye-opening still. I met face-to-face with more people who had experienced things I couldn't imagine.

Since visiting Tibet and living in India for three years, I have been privileged to work with Tibetans in a variety of settings, at various charity dinners celebrating Tibetan culture and the Tibetan spirit, publishing editorials and feature articles in newspapers and magazines, marching at protests and demonstrations, and even during a two-month Trans-America Run for Dignity and Human Rights that took me on foot more than 1,500 miles from San Francisco to Colby, Kansas. These opportunities have afforded me the chance to talk with and interview dozens of Tibetans with torture experience inside Chinese prisons.

These are the stories that have been preserved in this book. These are the interviews, a testament of Chinese brutality that is just a few pages away, in black and white, for the world to see.

The ambassador's call had been a good one. I went to see for myself, and this book is the result. I must thank him someday for the suggestion.

JAMYANG LODROE

Jamyang Lodroe was born in Lhasa in 1956. His father joined the Four Rivers, Six Ranges Khampa resistance movement in 1959, and to this day he does not know whether his father has died or if he is alive. His mother died due to Chinese police torture in 1962. In 1975, he tried to escape to India but was caught. This was followed by more than six months of solitary confinement, accompanied by beatings and torture of considerable brutality. He participated in the 1989 independence demonstrations in Lhasa; two of his friends were killed and he was arrested and tortured. He finally escaped to India in October 1993, reaching Dharamsala in November of the same year. Jamyang Lodroe works as a driver.

WHEN THE CHINESE took over Tibet in 1959 I was three years old. My aunt later told me that four members of my family joined the Tibetan resistance movement, called Four Rivers, Six Ranges during that year; my father was one of them. I have no memory of ever having seen my father and to this day do not know whether he is alive or not.

My mother stayed in Lhasa to look after us children. She taught me how to read and write. In 1962 she was caught helping other Tibetans by writing letters for them to their relatives. She was tortured very badly and died the same year. The responsibility for my upbringing fell on my maternal aunt and her husband.

In 1965 I went to school. Two years after that my uncle was arrested by the Chinese police after they searched our home and found some weapons and some old Tibetan currency. Our house was plundered; except for blankets and kitchen utensils, everything was taken away. In the same year some Chinese officials ordered me to shout anti-America slogans. But, already seething with rage for what the Chinese did to my home and to my uncle, I instead shouted: "On Live America!" For this, I was expelled from school. My fellow students were made to go around the Barkhor shouting, "Americans Go Back!" I never understood what this slogan meant. Go back from where?

After being expelled from school I was sent to a spinning mill where I had to produce woolen yarn. I hated this work. I did not consider this a man's job. Nevertheless, I was forced to remain at this job for a year and a half. After that I was sent to work at the Toelung Electric Power Station. But I did not know anything about electricity and the manager of the station told me to take driving lessons. I did, and was eventually employed to drive the power station vehicle. I remained at this job until 1974.

I was not very happy in Toelung and earned very little money. I started with a salary of eight mao (ten mao = one yuan) per day. This was later increased to one yuan.

* * *

In 1975 I returned to Lhasa on the pretext that I was ill and had to go to the hospital there. After my permit for staying in Lhasa expired my work unit leader at Toelung wrote to the relevant Neighborhood Committee in Lhasa, asking them to order me to return to Toelung. But I did not want to return and planned to escape to India. I made the plan with four others: Thundup, Norbu, Masasi (a Tibetan Muslim) and Wangchen. We stole a jeep and drove towards the border. But our plan failed when Nunu accidentally drove the jeep into a ditch. We had no choice but to abandon the jeep and return to Lhasa.

Wangdu had not turned up when we set out to Lhasa and I suspected that he would inform the police.

After we returned to Lhasa we were arrested on January 31, 1975. We were handcuffed and taken to the main PSB (Public Safety Bureau) station in Lhasa. When we arrived there, Wangdu was just coming out. We felt angry and during interrogation we told the interrogators that Wangdu was the main organizer of the escape plan. That led to his arrest. All five of us were taken to Gutsa prison.

* * *

On arrival at Gutsa we were severely beaten. I was nicknamed Hutug (son of nobles), which implied that I was a pampered upper-class boy. I was accused of having links with ten other hutugs But I steadfastly maintained that I never had any connection with them. In the end ten hutugs were executed.

I was kept in a solitary cell for six months and twelve days. On one occasion my friend Nunu tried to escape from prison with a Mongolian boy. But they were caught and taken back to their cells. After this incident all political prisoners were hand and leg-cuffed for some time.

Every night we were interrogated and asked whether we had any links with a certain underground resistance movement. And every time we denied it we were beaten with rifle butts or suspended from the ceiling by our hands, which were tied behind our backs. The same questions were asked each time. Once I got so desperate that I tried to kill myself by jumping on a knife which one of the interrogators was holding in his hand. But I failed and only ended up getting even more beatings. They told me: "We will not allow you to die."

* * *

On August 12, 1975, the guards read out the names of eight prisoners. One of them was mine. We were called up, our handcuffs were removed and we were given some food. We thought we were going to be executed. Nunu and the Mongolian boy started crying from fear of death. After we had finished eating we were taken to a large playground. Two guards accompanied each one of us. We were put in self-tightening hand and leg-cuffs and made to stand on a stage facing a large crowd. A wooden board was hung around each of our necks which read *hengdhu Sarje Ngologpa* (modern counter-revolutionary). We had to listen to our rimes being read aloud. We were accused of forming a counter-revolutionary association and of making an illegal attempt to escape. Our sentences were announced.

* * *

Nunu was sentenced to seven years of imprisonment. Tenzin was given five years. Onosi was black-capped (declared a social outcast) for three years. I was black-capped for six years. However, Wangdu was released without any punishment. Thereafter Nunu and Tenzin were taken back to prison. Onosi and I were handed over to our Neighborhood Committee, which made us sign a document stating we would not leave anywhere without prior permission. Even when leaving our house we were bound to inform our neighbors of our destination. If we wanted to stay at someone's home for a number of days we had to inform our Neighborhood Committee. Every morning we were required to sweep the surrounding areas. We had to report immediately whenever the Neighborhood Committee called us to do some work. Sometimes we were sent to collect human feces. This work did not entitle us to any pay. It was only when the Neighborhood Committee did not have any work for us that we could go and work at the yarn factory to earn some money.

In 1979 all the black-capped ones had their black-caps

removed and many political prisoners arrested in 1959 were released. A new era began. Under this new liberty I applied for a job at the Lhasa City Transport Company. They accepted me and employed me as a bus driver.

* * *

Though I took part in demonstrations in Lhasa in 1987 and 1988 I was not involved in organizing them. But in 1989 I formed a small group intending to take part in a demonstration, which was being planned for March 1989. Tsegog-la and I led the group. During the demonstration two of my friends were killed. Ani was shot dead on March 6. Dawa Tsering was beaten to death on the street by armed police (Chinese: wujing) on March 5. Pa Tsengo was arrested on March 8, and I was arrested a day later.

I was taken to my home in the middle of the night. I was kicked and beaten with rifle butts at the time of my arrest. My hands were tied behind my back and I was taken to the police station where again I was kicked and beaten, especially in my face. After some time I was taken to another police station where again I was beaten. I was asked to give the names of other people in my group. First I denied that I had taken part in the demonstrations at all. But when the police confronted me with still and video pictures of me participating in the demonstration, I had to admit that I did take part in the demonstrations. Still I insisted that I only watched the demonstrators and that I had not really taken part in the demonstration. At this I was kicked very hard in my kidneys. Since then my kidneys have been constantly troubling me. The interrogators also applied an electric cattle prod to my face, neck and hands. They also used some kind of electric gloves with which they pinched me in the face. This was very painful. I was finally dragged into a cell and left there, lying on the ground, almost unconscious. Other prisoners helped me onto a bed. Around 4:00 a.m. I was taken to Outidu Prison, Sangyip.

* * *

In Outidu I was put in a cell outside the prison compound. I was given a mug and a pair of chopsticks. In the morning I got two hard ingmo (steamed bread) and a cup of black tea. There was no lunch. On the evening of March 12, the prisoners in my cell did not get any food. I lost my temper and threw my chopsticks in the air. They hit my mug on the window sill which then clattered with a loud noise to the concrete floor. Fellow prisoners felt encouraged and also threw their chopsticks in the air. The guard came and soon found out that I had started this incident. I was beaten until I felt numb.

On March 14, I was taken to the Old Seitru Prison, Sangyip. I was put in a cell with four others and left alone for one month without being beaten or interrogated. Then three TAR officials—one Chinese and a male and female Tibetan—came to interrogate me. Again I was asked to give the names of fellow demonstrators. On the first day I was not beaten. But on the subsequent days I was tortured every day.

* * *

I was stripped naked and made to kneel on a wooden stick. After some time my knees started to hurt very much. Two PSB (Public Security Bureau) men gave me electric shocks on my genitals. This sort of treatment continued and my health deteriorated considerably after some days.

One morning I met Pa Tsengo while I was going to the toilet. We quickly exchanged some information. I learned that my friend too was being treated in much the same way. He, too, was very weak.

One day a PSB man came into my cell carrying a stiletto. He threatened to kill me if I did not give him any names of people

14

in my group. When I refused the PSB man stabbed me in my thighs: twice on the right leg and once on the left. I was left without treatment for two days. I could not move my legs. My cellmates started appealing to the authorities to take me to the hospital. Finally I was taken to the prison dispensary.

The dispensary had one doctor and he was a Chinese man. He stitched my wounds and treated me for three months and sixteen days. At first I tried to tell him what caused my wounds, but he warned me to keep quiet in order to avoid more problems.

* * *

I spent the last seven days of my prison life in the old Seitru from where I was finally released without being tried or sentenced. I went straight to my aunt's house. But she had just died from the agony of hearing about my ill treatment in prison.

Soon after my release I was called to the Neighborhood Committee where I was made to sign several documents understanding not to take part in any more demonstrations. They took seven passport-size photographs of me and also my thumbprints. Thereafter, I went to the Transport Company where I used to work before my arrest. But the head of the company told me he could not employ me officially since I had taken part in demonstrations. He proposed to hire me on a casual basis. I turned down the offer and found employment as a truck driver with a businessman from Kham. My job was to transport goods between Lhasa and destinations in Kham.

* * *

On May 24, 1993 my neighbors came to my house and warned me not to take part in the demonstration, which would take place that day. I decided to stay at home to avoid trouble. However, when my children came back from school that afternoon I changed my mind. They were crying and told me that the police had thrown tear gas bombs in their schoolyard (The Barkhor Junior School). I felt very angry and encouraged my neighbors to go out and take part in the demonstration. I convinced them and we all went. When we reached the site, the demonstrators had just started shouting independence slogans in front of the Potala Palace.

My neighbors and I marched along with the demonstrators towards the main TAR Government Office complex. While some people were shouting slogans about prices rising others were shouting slogans for independence. The situation was very chaotic. I shouted slogans saying "Free Tibet."

After three days the police came to my house to look for me. They asked me if I had encouraged my neighbors to go to the demonstration. I replied that I had indeed done so, but that we did not raise any slogans calling for independence. The police did not say anything and left. They did not come back.

In August 1993 I received a call from my former employer, the Lhasa City Transport Company. The manager told me that the office could sell me a truck on an installment basis of 800 yuan per month if I was interested. However, I was told that I could use this truck on one condition: wherever I went somebody would always accompany me from the office. I accepted the offer and from that moment onwards I made regular trips to Kongpo. I transported wood from Kongpo to be sold in Lhasa.

The person who accompanied me seemed quite friendly. Once I confided in him that I put up independence posters in Che Dzong in Dege, Kham in November 1991. I told him that I did it because the locals in the village were not willing to take such risks. Rather than standing up against the Chinese, they promptly obeyed any orders barked by them. A primary school teacher followed my example and put up some posters as well.

He was arrested immediately. I never learned his name and I do not know what happened to him after his arrest.

Shortly after I had told my colleague about the incident in Kham, I was called to the office which had mortgaged me the truck. I was asked what I had done in Kham. I denied everything and was let off without any more trouble.

* * *

One day I found myself in Shigatse without anything to be loaded in my truck; I had just unloaded a cargo of iron bars. I therefore stayed back for some time looking for goods to be transported. I soon found work when a Tibetan man asked me if I would carry a cargo of vegetables for him to the border town of Zangmo for 1,500 yuan. But I did not have the special pass to go to that border town and told him so. At this he took a passport size photograph from me and soon got a pass made for me. I told the person appointed to accompany me that I would go to Gyantse to look for cargo and that I would be back very soon.

I left in the evening of that day in October 1993. I asked one of my friends in Zangmo whether he could find me a guide who would take me across the border to Nepal. Not long afterwards my friend came back with a Nepali woman who said she would take me to Nepal for 1,200 yuan. I decided to go with her and take the chance.

I wrote a letter to the office that had mortgaged me the truck, saying I was going to India and that they could pick up their truck from Zangmo. At that time I did not think of the risk my escape would entail for my wife and children. Only later did I realize that my action might have put them in trouble.

I left Tibet with three guides and two other escapees who had each paid only 800 yuan. I realized that I should have bargained with the guide. We reached Barabisi without much trouble. It happened to be Diwali (the Hindu New Year Festival) when we arrived. We therefore could not leave for Kathmandu immediately as there was no bus. We spent our time learning some Nepali. We left for Kathmandu as soon as the buses started running again.

I reached Dharamsala, India, in November 1993.

JAMPA PHUNTSHOK

Jampa Phuntshok is 71 years old. His parent's house was in Penpo, north of Lhasa. He had 4 brothers and one sister. He and his brothers all became monks, but though his brothers all entered Drepong Monastery, Jampa Phuntshok joined Sera. Soon afterwards he changed to Namgyal Monastery - the monastery of His Holiness, the Dalai Lama, located in the Potala Palace. He lived and studied at Namgyal for 11 years.

AT THE SAME time that I entered [Namgyal] monastery, His Holiness had just been brought to Lhasa from his birthplace in Omdo. As I was the youngest monk in Namgyal, I used to be the playmate of H.H., the Dalai Lama.

When I was 32 years old, in 1959, the Chinese Army invaded Tibet. When the attack began in Lhasa, many of us took off our robes and prostrated before the empty throne of the Dalai Lama. We took the weapons stored in the Potala. Outside, thousands of Tibetans had gathered to protect the Dalai Lama from the Chinese. When we heard that the Dalai Lama had escaped safely, we were very happy. But then we wondered what to do. Some of us had weapons, but the Chinese Army was strong. We argued and discussed what we should do. Some argued, "We should stay and protect the Potala Palace." Others said, "No, the Chinese will just bomb it from airplanes and destroy what we are trying to save. The Potala is too precious. We can't let it be destroyed. Better to leave it." So we left the Potala and split up into groups. I went with a group to the north, toward Penpo. Along the way, I felt I should stop to see my mother. The group's leader told me I shouldn't go, but

I went anyway. Once at my mother's home, she told me not to leave again. She worried I would be killed. I could never disobey my mother. My teachers, my father, I sometimes disappointed everyone, but not my mother. So I stayed home. Other monks who had also decided against fighting, left me their weapons. My house was like an armory. Some people came to stay with us, and we all tried to help the resistance fighters any way we could. A guerilla leader came to my house one day. His name was Sangphel, and before the fighting, he had been a famous bandit, a highwayman. He had found out somehow that I had weapons, and asked for them. I gave him what he asked for, but I made him sign a receipt. If our government was restored, I wanted to make sure the weapons could go back in the Potala where they belonged.

After a time, I left home and joined Sangphel's group. There were many resistance groups. The guerillas made good use of the rough territory which we knew well. We traveled north to some snow mountains. We planned to hold the pass through the mountains and make it impossible for the Chinese to move through that area. There were 500 of us together, but really we didn't have very much ammunition, and food was scarce. There was much indecision. We talked about escaping to India. Some people thought the climate and culture would be too different there. There were also rumors that the Americans were going to help us. We decided to stay, thinking, "If we can last a little longer, the Americans will come."

Eventually we saw an airplane. Sangphel said not to shoot, it was an American airplane and would drop supplies. But it didn't drop any supplies, it was Chinese. They spotted us and sent soldiers. Many Chinese soldiers came, forty Tibetans were killed in the battle. The rest of us escaped through the mountains, most of us on horseback. But again the Chinese airplanes found us and the soldiers followed. Sangphel was badly wounded, he said he couldn't go on and was going to surrender. So we left Sangphel and split up into small groups to escape the soldiers.

I was with ten others. A storm of rain and hail hid us from the Chinese Army and we escaped through the mountains. Keeping to the high land we traveled here and there, avoiding soldiers and getting what food we could find. There were many airplanes, and we knew the Chinese would see us eventually. One day I woke with a bad feeling, with butterflies in my stomach. That morning I spotted soldiers in the distance. Our position was strong and we decided to stay and fight. There were hundreds of soldiers. There were only eleven of us, but none of us were killed. In the afternoon, we ran out of ammunition. Then we fled. Dropping our weapons, everything, we just ran, getting away however we could. Four of us were still together, two of my brothers and another monk. I began to worry about my mother. Our house was well known as given refuge to people fighting the Chinese. As we traveled, we asked for news of Penpo. One day we met some nomads and stayed with them. One nomad, who had recently been to Penpo, actually knew about my house. He said that the Chinese had taken my parents and my sister. The nomad said that all their trouble came from one son, a monk from Lhasa, who had used the house as guerilla headquarters. The nomad didn't know it, but the son he was referring to was me. Hearing this and thinking I was the cause upset me. The nomad said that if the son surrendered, the Chinese would release his family members.

The Chinese announced that if we surrendered, nothing would happen to us. We would be forgiven as long as we caused no more trouble. I left the camp for a few days, to meet a relative secretly. My relative was a few days late, and when we met he told me my brothers had just surrendered. When I heard that, I gave myself up. When I surrendered in Penpo, the authorities were very nice. They said, "No problem." They released my mother, but our sister had been taken to Lhasa and was not released. One of my brothers, who also joined guerillas in the south of Tibet, was captured and imprisoned. When we first returned home, there were no problems. My mother was suspicious and told me that I shouldn't have surrendered, I should have kept fighting. But I told her I was tired of fighting. There were so few of us and so many Chinese, we could never kill them all. After one month, things began to change. The authorities started making accusations. They came to our house and found our supply of barley. They said, "Keeping barley is the same as keeping guns," and they took it all. They said we were wealthy landowners before and had oppressed the people. They said my brothers and I had killed many Chinese soldiers. They arrested the three of us and evicted my parents from their house. The Chinese took everything. They said it belonged to the people. My parents moved into the barn and my father begged for food to survive. Soon after he died of depression from losing all his six children.

In the beginning they left me alone in prison, but tortured and interrogated my brothers. After one month they began interrogating me. They questioned me about my part in the burning of a Chinese office. For four months they questioned me. They hung me by my arms and beat me. When they took me down, they chained my arms and legs close together so I could not stand. Many, many prisoners died in this time of torture or starvation.

I was in this detention prison for one year. Every day, when not being interrogated, we worked in the fields. The Chinese told us, "In the past you monks made everyone work for you, now it is your turn to work." One of our jobs was to carry the waste from the toilets and spread it in the fields. The Chinese knocked the heads off Buddha statues and made us use them as buckets. We used thangka paintings as pads on our backs when we carried the buckets. We were all so hungry during this time that we scrounged pieces of root, or bones we found to try and get something out of them. We also ate worms and insects.

After one year in detention, I was sentenced to 24 years, for killing soldiers and supplying weapons to the resistance. One of my brothers also got 24 years and the others 10 and 9 years. My sister was sentenced to 20 years. Chained together with twelve others, I was taken to Lhasa. A little north of the city, a monastery had been made into a prison called Bari Prison. After one year in Bari, I was moved along with some others to Penpo. At Penpo we were subjected to Thamzing. Thamzing is a "struggle session." A few people were picked out to confess their crimes against the people, and the people supposed to punish the offenders. The Chinese would taunt the people being "struggled." They make them denounce the Dalai Lama. They said things like, "If the Americans are so strong, where are they? Call them, see if they come and help you." Or they'd tell monks to call the deities they believed in to come and help them. Sometimes people were "struggled to death." My mother was also killed during a struggle session.

In Penpo prison we worked in the fields. There were not any draft animals and we did all that kind of work ourselves. There were many rumors that the Americans were going to help us. One rumor was that the Dalai Lama was returning and that the Tibetan flag was already flying from the Potala. The Chinese heard these rumors too. They beat up the people they thought were spreading them. I didn't get much damage, but others were in bad shape.

In 1965, I was taken to another prison for a year where I worked making bricks. All prisoners got a copy of "The Thoughts of Mao." The guards said those who could not memorize it were against Mao. Since I was a monk I was used to memorizing, in fact I liked memorizing and it was quite easy for me. Soon I could quote from the book perfectly. Then they said I must really like Mao. I didn't say anything. The other inmates weren't too happy with me. The guards used me as an example, asking others "Look what he did, why can't you do that?" Since the authorities praised me, other prisoners thought there must be something wrong with me. But my purpose was not to cause trouble, just to stay out of trouble. It was actually useful. When the guards caught me praying to myself, I would just say I was reciting Mao's book.

In 1966 the Cultural Revolution started. Chairman Mao wanted to eliminate the Four Olds, as he called it, old culture, old thoughts. The Chinese denounced everything about Tibet. They called the Dalai Lama a criminal. They banned incense, long hair, New Year celebrations, all our customs. All Tibetan writings were destroyed and replaced with Chinese. We have a custom in Tibet, of adding "la" to the end of a person's name when we address them, as a title of respect. The Chinese said we could not even do that anymore. They said we had to become Chinese. The monks had to dye their robes black, and could no longer call themselves monks. Wearing the colors maroon or saffron was banned altogether. In the prison, we burned scriptures as fuel. Once a week we had meetings to denounce the Dalai Lama. This was very difficult, as the Dalai Lama is my root guru. I felt as if all things I did were negative actions.

In 1966 I went to Kongpo prison, where I stayed until 1984.

This was a big prison, and we did all kinds of work; I worked in the metal shop for a while and at cutting trees. In 1978 I was given the job of tending the pigs. I had more freedom as I got outside the prison when I took the pigs out to forage.

In 1979 a delegation from the Dalai Lama came to Tibet. The leader of the delegation was one of His Holiness' brothers, Lobsang Samten. I wanted to meet him. I found out that they were going to visit Kongpo county. I needed something to take as a gift so I picked out the best apples meant for the pigs. Then I ran away from the prison. When I got to the town of Kongpo, I saw the shops were freshly stocked and the people well dressed. The Chinese were dressing the place up. I went to the place where the delegation was going to be. I was careful not to get caught. I didn't want to get caught before I met the delegation. If I got caught later, it didn't matter. When I got there, I didn't see anyone, so I hid in the toilet. When I could hear they'd arrived, I went out. I went to Lobsang Samten and told him who I was. When he recognized me he was overjoyed. We had been together as children at Namgyal monastery. We talked about some of our memories. I told him how we had to denounce the Dalai Lama in prison and that I felt bad. I came because I wanted to apologize. He said he had heard this before and he understood everything. We took a picture together before I left. I wanted to ask him for a picture of the Dalai Lama, but I knew the guards would take it away from me when I got back to the prison. When I returned to the prison, no one said anything to me. Later there was a gathering of prisoners and I was denounced. They said "Someone here is harming us, taking pictures with enemies of the people. Other prisoners were told to keep an eye on me.

The reason that I wasn't punished too much was that the Dalai Lama's brother had told me, in front of soldiers, to

25

contact him if I was mistreated. So the Chinese knew it would be bad propaganda for them. The Chinese announced that Tibetans in exile could come to Tibet and visit their relatives. They were trying to improve the image of Tibet.

In 1984 my sentence was over. I thought that after twenty-four years in prison, I was not a monk anymore. First I had taken up arms against the Chinese. During prison I had tried to satisfy them. I suffered for all this and felt selfish. I went to Penpo for a little while and stayed with my aunt. My sister who survived a 20 year prison term lived in a shabby hut like a toilet. Two of my four brothers died in prison due to torture and starvation. We lost everything we had before the Chinese invasion. Then, in 1985, I went to a place near Lhasa where people go on retreat. I stayed in meditation there until 1987. When I heard about the Drepung monks demonstrating in September, I liked this very much. I was doing spiritual practice, but felt I needed to be active, to do something for Tibet. The monks had sacrificed themselves for Tibet's freedom. I thought of all the time I had wasted in prison, the troubles I had caused myself. I became determined to do something and began praying that I could get the strength to do something. I began to practice shouting, so that when the time came my voice wouldn be a pitiful squeak.

In 1988 the Chinese allowed the New Year's Monlam festival for the first time in a very long time. I heard that monks from Ganden where planning something and thought this was good. But the monks were very young; if they went to prison their lives would be wasted. I was already old, so I thought I should do something; if I went to prison, it wouldn't be so bad as I was used to prison.

The Prayer Festival started on March 3. I dressed in a very nice monk's clothes, and did some circumambulations to get prepared. I went and put myself in the very center of the crowd.

During the ceremony I began to be afraid. But I decided, it doesn't matter, this is what I came to do. So I got up and threw some dried flowers into the crowd and shouted, "Long live His Holiness the Dalai Lama. Freedom for Tibet." Some others in the crowd began shouting as well. I saw some foreigners taking pictures so I did it again, threw the flowers and shouted for the cameras' benefit. Then I began to sing the Prayer for Truth, composed by the Dalai Lama, which is the Tibetan national anthem. I knew if I started this others would follow, because it was usual for one monk to lead other people in chanting. They followed for a while, and some shouted, but slowly it began to quiet down as people became afraid and ran off. I sat down, more or less content. I felt fulfilled, as if a big burden had been lifted. I thought the Chinese would come to get me at any time. After everyone left, I kept my seat. But no one came. So I returned to my place in the mountains.

I had a very auspicious dream that night. I was walking to the Potala, then I met His Holiness on the roof who patted me on the shoulder. I had a white piece of cloth and went down to where monks were doing puja and began spreading out the cloth. I took this as a sign that my sins were purified.

The Chinese hadn't tried to arrest me at the demonstration, but were looking for me. They took my photograph around to the monasteries, but of course no one knew me. Friends of mine came to visit and told me to run away, but I didn't want to. I told them it's no use to run away. Here I am by myself, if I go somewhere to hide, others will be implicated. The reason the Chinese left me alone was that very few people had joined me. They announced that one person tried to disrupt the ceremony, but no one supported him. The Chinese were confident that the population was afraid, and no trouble would come.

On March 17, three Chinese came to see me. They made an

excuse, but I knew why. Later about ten soldiers came. One took out a picture of me shouting, and asked if I knew who this was. I said, "Yes, it's me. I've been waiting for you." They searched my room. I said, "I have nothing here." They handcuffed me behind the back, walked me down the mountain to a waiting car and took me to Sietru prison.

At prison they said I have been here too many times, this is very bad. They shocked me with an electric prod. They put me into a little cell and said "This is where you'll stay for the rest of your life." I thought that was okay, I did what I had to do and it was enough. I kept doing my prayers, mantras and meditation. Again they came to ask me questions. One was a Tibetan. They took me to an interrogation room and asked personal details. Then: "Was your other prison term too short?" They asked what I shouted.

I said, "Long live His Holiness the Dalai Lama and Freedom for Tibet."

They asked, "How can you say 'Freedom for Tibet' there's no such thing. That was all in the past."

I said, "I was in Lhasa when the Dalai Lama was brought as a boy. It wasn't Chinese that brought him in, it was Tibetans. From my own experience, I know Tibet was free."

They listened to my long explanation and wrote it down. They asked, "Who got you to do demonstration?"

I said, "No one. I did it on my own."

They asked, "Why do you want freedom?"

I said, "If we don't have freedom, it is finished. We Tibetans feel like servants. Everything in Tibet is Chinese. All the rulers are Chinese. It is called Tibet, but even Tibetan language is useless."

They said, "Well, you are not very capable, that is why you are servants. We are capable and run this country for you. You want freedom, but no one is going to help you, not America, not Europe. No one accepts freedom for Tibet. No one can help you except us."

This went on like this once a week for two years and four months. They didn't interrogate me during my last six months. I wanted to go to India to be with His Holiness, but I was afraid I would be a burden. My friends persuaded me to come, so I could tell people about Tibet and what happens there.

So I came to India, and I am very happy to be at Namgyal Monastery once again. And I am happy I have been able to talk to you. I ask you to pass on some of what I have told you, so that people in your countries will know what is happening in Tibet.

DAPHLA

Dhapla was born in 1957, in Meta-ghong-ga, Tibet. He worked as a civil engineer for the Chinese government designing blueprints for hydroelectric plants, roads, and bridges in Tibet. He went to school in Tibet during the Cultural Revolution and spent four more years in China. He was never given a chance to finish his formal education. He was arrested on March 22, 1988 for hanging pro-independence posters and was detained for four years, released on March 22, 1992. Dhapla fled Tibet on April 5, 1996 and arrived in Dharamsala on April 22, 1996.

I WENT TO school for nine years during the Cultural Revolution. There was a lot of tension between the Tibetans who were divided for or against the Chinese occupation, and education was consequently inadequate. I did not want to attend school in China, but was advised by my parents that a formal education was the only means to becoming financially successful. I went to Rang-shi-ring in China to study for four years but after leaving wasn't given a chance to finish my education. I was forced to work as a civil engineer and was sent to Meta-gong-ga to work.

I worked as a civil engineer from 1974 until 1988. During this time I was appointed the position of second-in-command, inferior only to the Chinese government. I was eager to learn about the situation of Tibet before Chinese occupation. I would read books on Tibet's history during work breaks, and my employer would tell me not to read those books, that they were lies. My Chinese coworkers would tell me how the Tibetans

30

lived in poverty before 1959, and how the Chinese are their saviors. They told me that I should praise Communist efforts and work for them.

The Chinese would collect musk and medicinal herbs in the forest and sell the goods in the markets as a side-job. Tibetans were not allowed to do this. Hunting is illegal but Chinese government officials would hunt.

In my village there are forty Chinese offices and three Tibetan [ones]. The department heads were all Chinese. The Chinese publicize that Tibetans have a lot of power, but in reality they are all suppressed by the Chinese who have the ultimate power.

I saw corpses on the streets during the Monnlam Festival in Lhasa. After these sights of Chinese carrying beaten and bloody Tibetan corpses through the streets, I pledged to myself that I would rebel against the Chinese. I hung three posters, two in Tibetan and one in Chinese. I posted these on the door of the High Court. After two days, I posted another on the U-May, the District Director door. Another seven days later, I posted a Chinese letter on the Chinese offices in my village. I then took a vacation to Cham-du. The posters declared Tibet as an independent country and from that day onward, all Tibetans should work towards independence and work to get His Holiness back in Tibet. I declared myself a rebel (without a name) and would fight for Tibet's freedom. I posted the signs during the night and thought that no one had seen me. I was cautious, but internally I sacrificed myself for the sake of Tibet's independence and was prepared to bear any consequences.

One month after I posted the signs the Chinese arrested me. I was on a business trip to Thop-tong, seven hours from my home. I was surveying and four Chinese police called me and asked me some questions. I went to get my luggage and the Chinese said that if I cooperated that I would be released, but I knew that I was caught. I was taken aside, and without any resistance I went with the police to Meta-kong-gah.

At the police station, I was put into a dark room and interrogated. Both Chinese and Tibetan policemen interrogated me and continued to ask who else was involved. I insisted that I was the only one involved. The Tibetan police didn't beat without the Chinese, they would just stare at me. I was given a choice to either accept that Tibet was a part of China, or, imprisonment. If I wished to be released, I must tell my relatives, monks, and nuns that Tibet is a part of China. They showed me books that gave "proof" that Tibet has been a part of China for two thousand years. I refused to say that Tibet had ever been a part of China. I thanked the Chinese for my years of salary and for allowing me to work for Tibet by building bridges and roads. Also that I was glad I had a chance to work for the improvement of Tibet, but that Tibet is an independent country from China. On March 22, 1988 I was taken to Ghutsa prison. The Chinese were legally only allowed to keep me for six months; I was kept for eleven months.

I [must be] careful to whom I talk with, and especially take precaution against journalists. I know that I might have to go back to Tibet because it is difficult for me to find work in India without citizenship.

I believe that it is more powerful to do independence work in Tibet than it is in India. I believe that it is a boost for the Tibetan people when Tibetans rally in Tibet.

After I was released from prison, I was given a job as a cashier at a gas pump. I was able to escape on a permit to pilgrimage. I walked five days over the mountains to Nepal.

KARGA

Karga was released in 1989 after spending twelve years in Minyag Runga Khang and Dartse-do prisons. After his release he went back to his home to find that his relatives had died and that their land had been given away. He roamed around for five years, trying to find a job. He was not educated and had no vocational training and was unable to find regular employment. He decided to escape to India to see His Holiness the Dalai Lama and to find employment. He arrived in Dharamsala during January 1994.

KARGA WAS BORN in 1956 in a village named Shepar, Dege Zong. His family was very poor, as the Chinese had taken most of their land, animals, and possessions in 1959. The land with which they were left was so small that the barley that it yielded could feed them for only six months of the year. Karga's family was considered very reactionary and had to wear a black-cap. Karga's uncle, Kesang Tsering, was shot, and his family was watched. In 1963, Karga's father, Ngawang Jampa, was arrested when he tried to burn incense on a hill (at that time it was forbidden to pray or express any cultural traditions) and was sent to Minyag Ranga Khang prison. Nobody was allowed to visit him and nobody knew how many years he had been sentenced. Karga and his relatives were not allowed to talk about him. One day they heard from an ex-prisoner that he had died in prison, 1969.

Karga could not go to school. Most of the time he was idle, as the land that they had left was so small that there wasn't much work to be done.

* * *

In 1977, Karga tried to stab Sankhu, the man who had killed his uncle, Kesang Tsering. (Sankhu was a beggar before the Chinese occupation. He had been given a gun and a title by the Chinese and killed many Tibetans.) Sankhu didn't die, and Karga was immediately arrested and sent to Rangakhang prison. There are twenty-two different prisons in the Rangakhang prison complex. There were both political and non-political prisoners who lived together. There were also some Chinese political prisoners. They didn't support Tibetan independence, but they opposed communism, and some of them had connections with Taiwan. When Karga entered into prison, there were about four-hundred prisoners in each prison, most of whom were Tibetan.

Karga was first sent to Dege-dzong prison. During the four months he was kept there he was beaten a lot with iron bars, kicked, suspended from the iron bars of a high window, and electrically shocked.

He was then sentenced to seven years for being a rebel. He was transferred to Rukchende for two months. In Rukchende he was severely disciplined to work at a stone carving site. He was beaten every time he became distracted. Most of the fellow prisoners were waiting for their sentences.

After two months Karga was sent to Tun-go-lo prison. Although his sentence had already been announced, he was still forced to come for interrogation sessions. During interrogations he was constantly asked about his views on Tibetan independence.

Karga and his fellow prisoners had to carry heavy loads of soil on their backs. The land around the prison was prepared for cultivation. The loads were very heavy, and many people had wounded and injured backs; prisoners rarely were allowed to get medical treatment.

* * *

After three years in Tun-go-lo prison, Karga and a friend tried to steal weapons from the guards. They planned to escape with these weapons. They were successful in stealing the weapons, but discovered that there were no bullets in the guns. They hid the weapons under a rock. Karga's friend Tsethen Choembel managed to escape, but Karga was caught. He was kept in Ton-go-lo prison for three days during which he was intensively interrogated. He denied flatly that he had stolen guns.

After three days he was sent to Rukchende. His hands were cuffed behind his back and his legs were shackled with heavy chains to the ground. He was interrogated each day, beaten with iron bars, given electric shocks all over his body, and kicked in his mouth and face. During most of the interrogation sessions, his hands were spread wide apart and cuffed to the walls.

He consistently denied that he had stolen weapons. After eight months, the authorities still had not produced any evidence. They suspected him, but decided that they couldn't force him to confess. He was not sent back to Ton-go-lo because he was considered a very serious case. He was transferred to Dartsedo prison. In prison his hands and legs remained shackled, and he did not have to work.

The discipline was extremely strict. He was not allowed to receive any visitors.

After two years and three months he was sent back to Rukchende. Shortly thereafter his friend Tsethen Choembel, who had escaped with the stolen weapons, was arrested after he fired shots in his village. During an interrogation session he confessed everything, including Karga's initial involvement. Karga's sentence was extended by five years and he was transferred to Chulepar where he stayed for four more years. He was no longer interrogated, but had to strenuously labor carrying soil and stones.

After four years he was sent to Sambesang to finish the last two years and eleven months of his sentence. He had a fight with a Chinese official in Chelapar prison, and was therefore transferred. His sentence was not extended.

* * *

When he was released, he went back to his hometown. He found that the commune-system had been abolished. The small plot of land, which had once belonged to his family, had been distributed among some villagers, after all his relatives had died or moved. Having no land and no relatives, Karga decided to leave. He went to Golo Chumale Olzong. He tried several different ways to make money, but found it difficult to make a living. He finally resorted to hunting, which only paid one thousand Yuan for one musk deer.

After one year of wandering around, he came to Lhasa. He did not find any work in Lhasa and had to live on the money that he had earned as a hunter. He went to the Tsuglhakhang (holiest shrine in Lhasa) every day to pray for forgiveness. He felt very guilty about having killed so many animals.

After he had lived in Lhasa for one year, he had not found a job and decided to flee Tibet. He left on October 12, 1993 with eleven other people to go to India. They didn't have enough money to pay a guide, so they secretly followed another group that traveled over the Himalayas with a guide.

Around Sharkainbu they were stopped by Nepali policemen

and taken to the police station. Karga was asked to take a handful of tsampa out of his bag and eat it. When they saw him eating, they took the bag away from him. All of their food and money was taken away from them and they were released.

Karga and his companions reached Kathmandu safely, and arrived in Dharamsala in January 1994.

YESHI DAMDUL

Interviewed Tuesday, July 9, 1996 at the Reception Center, Dharamsala. Yeshi Damdul is 26. He was born in Lokha (near Lhasa).

YESHI DAMDUL WAS born in Lokha. From the age of 11, he studied at a local school, which was attended mainly by Tibetan students. After studying for three years he was forced to leave the school due to his family's financial difficulties; his family could no longer afford to pay the school fees. Yeshi Damdul returned home to help out on his family farm. After one year, he joined the monastery at Sungrob Ling. As the number of monks at the monastery was limited to fifty, it was difficult to get admission. However, through the help of a monk who was his brother's friend, Yeshi Damdul managed to get admission to the monastery.

On the evening of March 10, 1989, Yeshi Damdul and five other monks put up political posters on the wall of the local Chinese government offices. The posters read, "On live His Holiness the Dalai Lama." Before the Chinese occupation, Tibet was a free country. Now we have no human rights and freedom. We need our freedom back. The posters also described how the Chinese treat political prisoners. On the evening of March 15, 1989, once again they hung such posters. They were spotted by the night security guard who reported them to the high officials.

On March 16, 1989, a van full of Chinese army and police officers carrying guns arrived at the monastery. A car full of Tibetan officials carrying pistols accompanied them. They surrounded the monastery. Several came inside and forced all the monks into one hall. They asked who put up the posters. When no one answered, they searched several of the monks' quarters. They threw the monks' belongings everywhere, looking for evidence such as pro-independence literature. Those who had letters from friends or family abroad were suspected. The police beat several monks, threatening to kill them if they did not give the names of those who had hung the posters. The police beat the monks with their guns. Eventually ten monks (including Yeshi Damdul) and one old woman who had shouted, "Tibet is a free country!" were taken to Tsetan prison for further interrogation. Two nuns from Shungseb and two monks from Samyal were also there. They were kept at Tsetam for eight months. Normally, prisoners can only be kept for six months before a sentence is declared. Yeshi Damdul was questioned daily. Four or five police officers would interrogate him in a small room. Most were Tibetan. Regardless of how he answered their questions, he was beaten. If he admitted to hanging the posters, he was beaten. If he did not admit to hanging the posters he was still beaten. He was also tortured with electric batons. After eight months, some of the prisoners were released. Others were sent to various prisons.

Yeshi Damdul was sentenced to four years and two months at Drapchi prison. At Drapchi, he was kept in a small room with about twenty other prisoners. The political prisoners were required to work seven hours a day growing vegetables. There were more restrictions on the political prisoners than on the others. For example, if a political prisoner had to go somewhere, a guard always accompanied him. Other prisoners were permitted to go alone. They were given food (mostly rice and flour) three times a day. Thirty-five yuan per month was allocated for each prisoner's food. As such, they did not receive meat and vegetables.

Once a week (on Saturdays), the prisoners were required to attend a seven-hour political re-education class. During these classes, they were told that the international community would never believe the lies of the Dalai Lama and that the Chinese would always challenge such lies. They were also given historical explanations for China's rule over Tibet. They were also told that they would be released if they admitted that Tibet is under China. However, not one prisoner accepted this offer.

Once in a month (on the 20th), the prisoners were permitted to receive guests. The guests could bring 7.5 kilos of food (usually tsampa). However, often they were only allowed several minutes with their family. Three police guards would watch and listen to their conversations. If they spoke softly, the police officers would instruct them to speak loudly. If the guests overstayed, both the prisoner and the guests would be beaten.

On April 27, 1991, the political prisoners were taken outside to work. When they arrived back at the prison, they noticed that five of their fellow inmates were missing. Several prisoners (including Yeshi Damdul) asked the guards where they were. The guards replied that inmates don't have the right to ask such questions. Out of concern for their missing friends, once again they asked the guards where they were. As a result, the army was brought into the prison and thirty prisoners received severe beatings. Their hands were tied and they were kicked and beaten with guns. As a result, many of them sustained broken bones and permanent health damage. Yeshi Damdul complains of chronic back pains and stomach problems, which he attributes to this beating. Two or three days later, it was discovered that the five missing prisoners had been transferred to another prison (Damo prison) in Kongpo.

Although Yeshi Damdul's family was never arrested, the police harassed them because of his political activites. Whenever something happened in their village, they were immediately suspected and blamed. Yeshi Damdul was released on March 17, 1994. Through a connection, he managed to get a job in the Department of Religious Affairs in Lhasa. He stayed there two years, but he was not happy at his work. He was always looked upon with suspicion. Although he did not participate in any big demonstrations, he was arrested and questioned twice. During these detentions he was not beaten and he was released after several days.

Yeshi Damdul traveled one day from Lhasa by bus. Then he walked one month and twenty days. He was traveling with a guide, ten children and one nun. They hid during the day and walked at night. By the time they reached the border, they had finished all of the tsampa. They asked the Nepalis for food. At Solo Khumbu, they met another group of Tibetans from Kham. They all traveled together to Kathmandu, accompanied by a Nepali police officer. They reached Kathmandu on a weekend and the offices were closed. They were therefore kept in prison for two days, together with the Nepali prisoners. They then stayed at the Reception Center for three days before being sent on to India. They arrived in Dharamsala on May 29, 1996.

TAMDIN TSERING

Tamdin Tsering was born in Rebong Zhophung Chi, Domed Amdo. He now works at the Department of Information and International Relations in Dharamsala.

FROM 1958 TO 1962 I studied Tibetan at the primary school at Rebong Zhophung Chi. From 1962 to 1966 I worked on the cooperative farm in my native place, from 1965 to 1996 as a cattle veterinarian. I became a member of the communist party of China in 1965. Between 1966 and 1969 I worked at the hydroelectric installation in the same place. Then, from 1969 to 1972 I studied at the Tsongon Higher Institute of Nationalities, majoring in Tibetan, with a minor in Chinese. In 1972 and 1973 I worked as a translator (Chinese-Tibetan) at the Nyinshug Xiang in Tsekhog Dzong. From 1973 to 1978 I was a police officer attached to the Public Security Bureau in Tsekhog Dzong. From 1978 to 1983 I was a deputy leader of the Regional Communist party of China at Tsekhog Dzong in Dokarmo Xiang. From 1983 to 1986 I was the senior Chinese Communist party leader of Chisa Xiang in Tsekhog Dzong, and had responsibilities in the political affairs of the dzong. From 1986 to 1988 I was the senior Chinese Communist party leader and political head at Tobden Xiang in Tsekhog Dzong. Between 1988 and 1990 I was the senior communist party leader and political head at Do-karmo Xiang and Tsekhog Dzong. From June 1990 I was the head of the Working Committee of the People Congress of Tsekhog, and the General Secretary of the Working Committee for nationalities affairs dealing with legal affairs. I escaped into exile on the eleventh day of the eighth month of the Tibetan calendar, falling in the year 1990.

I will first speak briefly about my family background. My father, Kunsang Tsering, was one of five children, and my mother, Sangye Tso, was one of seven children. Both of them belonged to the same clan and paternal heredity. There are only thirteen families who shared a common paternal descent with me. Our paternal ancestry has historically produced famous, religious, and powerful men. My paternal ancestors are known as the family of Zhophung Garwa. Such renowned men as Gendun Choephel came from my family. His works—an urn hand-made by him, a traditional Tibetan drawing-room desk made from red sandal wood which is an artistic wonder of much beauty and craftsmanship, a painting of KYILKHOR that he painted, and two volumes of his compositions—are now in my cousin's home. These escaped the communist onslaughts and can now actually be seen. I was born at my mother's place and brought up by my grandmother. My father's family was big, and was categorized by the Chinese as part of the rich serf-owning class. In 1958 the Chinese imprisoned my father along with three of his relatives and confiscated all their property, including houses, land, and herds. The children were left without anyone to look after them. I saw my father and four other older persons being suspended in air and being so mercilessly beaten that it was impossible to bear. At the same time, a novice tantric named Konchok Tashi was shot to death before a large arranged crowd. My father and his two other relatives arrested by the Chinese died in prison. Two of my mother's brothers also died in prison of starvation and torture.

My mother belonged to a middle propertied farming family. All her relatives and neighbors who were rich, well known, or influential were arrested by the Chinese and imprisoned. My family was blacklisted (made outcast). In 1959 my mother's two brothers were arrested, tied up, and subjected to humiliations and beatings. The UNNING DOGS of communist China interrogated them, "Since none of you and your relatives love the communist party of China, when do you intend to try to resurrect the ghost of the old social order? The communist party will chop off the heavenly abode of your existence, tumble it down, and replace it by the very root of the nether world of the snakes." Thus, my entire family was humiliated, imprisoned, and tortured. In January 1960, we, consisting of six family members, tried to escape to India through a monastic estate (Labrang). Unfortunately, we fell into the Chinese hands at the place called Amchog. Thereafter, so long as we could breathe and see, life for us was one of actual hell on earth. My grandmother starved to death while being taken to prison. Along with my mother, three cognates (consanguines) and I, then twelve years old, were taken to prison at a place called Kenlho. Being a child I felt slightly happy to be in prison, because I could eat one Tingmo (steamed dumpling) each day, which is difficult to get in the village. One of my mother's brothers, Kunchok Gyal, who was previously a monk, had tried to resist being tied up. In punishment he had his finger cut off with a knife, and for more than a month all three of them had their feet manacled by iron chains weighing about 12 kg each. In the third Tibetan month of the same year we were handed over to the Tsongon people militia. There we were fed very little, no more than 150 grams of ration per day. We ate grass, which grew between the crevices of stones, to supplement this ration. These three uncles used to give me part of their share of food, so that I could survive longer, as they had given up to live long. During the day prisoners had to work the land and at night they were beaten mercilessly by members of the people militia.

The militia interrogated and tortured them. Finally, on the 27th day of the fourth month of the Tibetan calendar in 1960, we were put on horses, which were given wild chase along rocky mountains. During the chase, my mother's three brothers met a violent death, and I alone survived.

In 1990, the Chinese under a proclaimed policy of recompense, paid 300 Yuan per deceased individual. This was a moment of very sad reflection for us about our deceased relatives—and the tragic end which they met. Moreover, it was humiliating to have to swallow the idea that they could try to compensate with such ease and cheapness so rare a thing as human life. This only enhanced our resentment. On both my father's and mother's side, nine of my relatives lost their lives. The red Chinese still bear stains of their blood.

* * *

In 1958, I was ten years old, and the Chinese sent a countless number of their troops into Tibet for a violent invasion. The Tibetans were subjected to hardships, which can be rarely imagined on this earth. We found ourselves in a situation devoid of all individual rights, no right to property or to land. Innocent persons, whether monks and lamas in the monasteries, or ordinary lay persons engaged in their respective chores, were robbed, imprisoned, and brutally slaughtered without any remorse. Even watch dogs were eliminated without a trace. I have personally experienced and witnessed these atrocities. In 1958, four lamas, six monks, and sixty-seven lay people of my villages were imprisoned although they were all innocent of any crimes. Of those, twenty-three died in prison, and one was directly killed. In my area there were 150 families, constituting 906 people. From 1959 to 1961, the Great Leap Forward was imposed on the Tibetans, and 267 people starved to death in my area alone. At that time a manual worker was given a ration of 300 grams of Tsampa (Barley flour) and children were entitled to 200 grams of Tsampa. To supplement our ration, we had to pick weeds from the fields to eat. We also had to eat a particular species of grass called Dumtsa Sogley, which grows on the rocky mountains of Amdo, and seeds of a species of grass called Rambhu. People were forced to boil all kinds of leather goods and bones in water and drink it. Many people today still have abdominal complications from these times. In that period of famine the Chinese, inexcusably, would punish any persons which they saw light a fire. If a Chinese person saw smoke coming out of a Tibetan house, he would report it to the authorities, who would search the house. If any grains were found, the members of the family would be tied up and paraded in public. The family was blacklisted and had to perform extra labor, for less food, which was of an even worse quality. Five Tibetans in my area committed suicide out of desperation.

In other parts of Tibet, a countless number of Chinese colonizers were sent under the name of planners and helpers to the Tibetans. In the Ziling area near Domed Tsongkha the Chinese population is 700,000 in the summer, and increases to 1.1 million in the winter. During the winter, more Chinese come to Ziling, which is warmer. The Chinese also carry out relentless exploitation of Tibet's mineral resources like gold, silver, copper, iron, aluminum, lead, uranium, coal, marble, and petroleum. They also take trees and herbs, otter, fish and birds. They plunder the whole of Tibet. They also take grains, oil seeds, yak meat, mutton, butter, cheese, milk, wool, leather, etc. The Tibetans were systematically deprived of everything they had by the Chinese, who transported everything to China. This was going on at the time I left Tibet.

The Chinese came to Tibet in 1958-59 with empty purses.

Now a single Chinese family owns a house of anywhere between seven and ten rooms. The poorest among them own a three-room house. A Chinese family returning to China goes home with anywhere between one to two railway bogeys full of Tibetan goods. This has also been confirmed to me by a patriotic Tibetan who I knew fairly well and who had been a deputy leader of the regional government at Tso-ngon region, Shagba. He was courageous person who confronted the Chinese face to face, and later died a sudden death.

* * *

Prior to 1978, the Chinese government used to levy a tax of five parts of a Yuan for the first grade of wool per half kilogram, four parts of a Yuan for the second grade, and three parts of a Yuan for the third grade; three Yuan for a sheepskin, thirteen Yuan for a sheep, and between forty and fifty Yuan for Yak, five parts of a Yuan for half kilogram of butter, and two Karma for a half kilogram of Milk. They extorted these taxes.

From 1988 on, the Chinese government started making compulsory purchases from the people and paying them mere pittances. For a half kilogram of wool 1.7 to 2.4 Yuan were paid; but when selling it to the public 13 to 14 Yuan were charged. For a sheep the Chinese government paid 40 Yuan, and then sold it to the public for 150 to 200 Yuan. For cattle the Chinese government paid 300 to 400 Yuan, and sold them for 700 to 1,000 Yuan. They paid 13-15 Yuan for an animal skin and sold it for 30-45 Yuan. If Tibetans were detected selling to private individuals rather than to the Chinese government, penalties were imposed. In the case of nomads, rates paid were 13 Yuan per half kilogram of wool, 105 Yuan for a sheep, and 971 Yuan for a cow. There were wool penalties, meat penalties, skin penalties, weed penalties, milk penalties, disciplinary penalties, staff penalties, counseling penalties, birth control penalties, project establishment penalties, etc. Thus, in one of the bigger Xiangs of the Rebgong nomadic region the collection of the wool penalty alone came around 1,300,000 Yuan in a year. Since 1988 taxes have become much heavier, including meat tax, cattle tax, production tax, filtered water tax, electricity tax, etc. For example, in Xiang, where I used to live, the cattle tax was raised in 1988 from 110,000 Yuan to 180,000 Yuan.

The Xiang of which I had been the head, is one of the largest in the Dzong. In it there were 115,157 sheep, 43,713 cattle, 2351 horses. There were 174,000 Mu (13 Khel, 1 Khel is 58 kilograms) of grain harvested. It is about 4,000 feet above sea level at the highest point, and 2,400 at the lowest. It is higher in the east and lower in the west. The area has a crop season of only about 110 days. The area has a population of 5,626. Of these, seventy-two are administrators. The administrative staff includes twenty communist party members and forty-five Tibetans. The twenty-seven Chinese made up thirty-four percent of the staff.

There were two schools in the area, with a total of only 158 students. The Chinese government allows very little funds for school. Consequently, of the 700 children of school going age, only 150 could be admitted. The Xiang has, in its entire history under communist Chinese rule, not witnessed a single student go on for higher studies. It is obvious that while the Chinese government wants Tibet's mineral resources, forests, animal products, herbs, and grains, they want to make sure that the Tibetan people do not become educated. They fear that well-educated Tibetans would learn to value their unique cultural heritage and thereby endanger the colonial communist Chinese political institutions. The Chinese government does not even attempt to give a good education to Tibetan children. This can be made out from the statement of Communist Chinese leader Deng Xiao Ping who talks of the flow of political power from the barrel of a gun, stating that here in the future, we shall have to be careful about campaigns by the nip of the pen. I personally have witnessed these obstacles to the education of Tibetan children.

Since I complained about the situation in Tibet mentioned above, and the discriminatory treatment of Tibetans at various meetings, large and small, the Chinese began to suspect my faithfulness on several points. There, I reluctantly had to escape to exile. I have always wished that as a Tibetan I should be able to serve the Tibetan nation in whatever way that I can, propagating its cause, under the leadership of His Holiness the Dalai Lama. It is with this end in view that I left behind everything—rank, pay, land, and children—and escaped into exile.

DAMCHOE

Damoche is 33 years old.

ON MARCH 3, 1989, I participated in the freedom demonstrations in Lhasa. Four days later on March 7, Public Security Bureau (PSB) officials came to my house in the night. Ten policemen came in and searched through my entire house. They broke into locked cupboards with their bayonets, and even searched through rice jars and food containers. Then they arrested me, my husband, and two monks who were in my house. One of those monks is now in Dharamsala also, Yeshe Togden, the president of the Gu-Chu-Sum Movement of Tibet.

The police interrogated me every day, usually from 9:00 am to 12:30 pm. These interrogation sessions included beatings with a bamboo stick. While they beat me they said things like: "What you did was stupid and wrong. You think America supports you, but you are wrong. They don't support you, no one supports you. You will never gain independence through this kind of activity." My family kept coming to Outridu to inquire after me, so the authorities transferred me to Gutsa Detention Center, which is very near by. After nine months, they released me after I signed a paper stating that I would never take part in such stupid activities again.

I was arrested again in May, 1993, three days after I and a few others had pasted flyers calling for Tibetan independence. Six PSB officials came for me at my shop near the center of Lhasa, and took me to my house. When we arrived there, the street in front was swarming with plain clothed police. We went inside where the police were ransacking my house. They searched for three hours, then took me to the nearest police station. They told me to give them the printing equipment. But I didn't have it. They thought maybe I had hidden it at my mother's house, and took me there while they searched. Then they took me back to my house and searched it again, insisting I must have the printing equipment somewhere.

Eventually they gave up and took me back to the police station. They made me stand in a cold room while they interrogated me. If I moved even an inch, they hit me. I told them I was four months pregnant. Despite my pleas, they kept me standing like that all night. Four men took shifts throughout the night, questioning me continuously. They demanded to know who had influenced my behavior and where I got the posters. When I did not tell them what they wanted, they beat me with whatever was handy, sticks, a padlock, their fists.

Around 3:00 am, four policemen took me in a car. There were more police in another car behind us. They said they were taking me to my execution, unless I told them who was behind my actions. Throughout this drive they hit me with their fists, slapped me, and pulled my hair. After an hour, we returned to the police station. They put me back in a cell, and the interrogation continued. Around 9:00 am, the four men left me to get breakfast, and a police woman came to the cell. She said I should sit down. I had been standing in the cold all night wearing only the thin clothes I had been wearing since the day before. I was like a stick— my joints were all stiff. I tried to sit down, but I fell and just lay there. I couldn't move an inch.

When the four policemen returned, they demanded to know why I was not standing up. They forced me to my feet and continued to question me. They kept punching me and pulling my hair.

Later they took me to the main police headquarters where

the interrogation continued. Later that day, they sent me to Sangyip Detention Center. My whole body hurt from the beatings. My scalp was like fire from my hair being pulled so hard.

At Sangyip prison, around midnight, I was taken to a small, dingy cell and strapped to a chair. They showed me photographs of many people. The police said they knew that I knew these people. They poked me in the face with a pen and other objects. They slapped me and asked me questions about the people in the photographs. They poked me with a cattle prod. They did not use the electricity on me, but kept the equipment in front of me to frighten me. They said, "We can do anything we want to you." They said they wouldn't give me any food. They made threats against my children and my parents.

I felt very weak. I told the officials I was pregnant and asked them to send me to the hospital. The police said I was lying and that I wasn't really pregnant. They said there wasn't time to take me to the hospital. They would take me after I answered my questions. When I told them what they wanted, then I could go to the hospital.

After four days they sent me to the police hospital. After my examination I heard the doctor telling the police that I was pregnant and very weak and should be admitted into the hospital. The police that were in charge of my case refused. They took me back to the detention center. At this time I could not keep food down, not even water. I vomited everything that I took. I kept asking to be taken back to the hospital, but was always refused. Four days later I miscarried in my cell. Prisoners in cells nearby called for the guards who found me. They carried me out of my cell and put me in the hospital. I had lost a lot of blood and was in shock. As soon as I was a little better, the police came and questioned me.

While I was in the hospital, my family was not informed about what had happened. After seven days I returned to Sangyip. The day after I got back, even though I was still very weak, the interrogation sessions continued.

The Chinese criminal procedure says that prisoners are to be sentenced within six months of their arrest and detention. I stayed in the detention center for ten extra months, contrary to Chinese law. Prisoners want their sentence because then they go to the regular prison and daily interrogations cease. In many cases, the police hold the prisoners much longer than six months so they can continue to interrogate them.

After one year and four months in Sangyip Detention Center, I finally went to court and was sentenced to three years. I was transferred to Drapchi prison, the only acknowledged prison in Tibet. There are many prisons, as Tibetans know, which authorities refer to as re-education camps, detention centers, and other names. In Drapchi, the political prisoners get different treatment than the other prisoners. Supposedly for health reasons, they made us do strenuous exercises throughout the day. Many of them were exercises done by Chinese army troops. Army personnel made us do these and other exercises. The People's Army Police, who guarded us, would casually beat and kick us as if it were nothing. We had to stand completely still for long periods, balancing a cup of water on our heads and holding a sheet of paper between our knees. They ordered us to look into the sun while exercising. Many prisoners fainted in the heat of the day. They made us sing, "I am a new person, reformed and able to meet any challenge." Some prisoners wouldn't sing and were punished with solitary confinement.

The authorities say that they make the prisoners exercise like this to keep them healthy. They say this is part of their concern for the prisoners, but this exercise is really a form of torture. Even on cold rainy nights they made us go outside and exercise. While I was in Drapchi, one nun got sick and died because of this.

My prison job was making yarn from wool. Each prisoner had a quota. If we didn't meet our quota, the guards made us work all night. All prisoners worked like this.

My sentence included two years of loss of political rights, following my release from prison. This is common for political prisoners. During these two years, the police closely monitored me. I had to check in with the police to travel even two kilometers from my home.

I came to Dharamsala to be an ambassador for Drapchi prison, and to tell the world what is happening. Even though many tourists come to Tibet, it is very difficult to speak with them. The police keep an eye on Tibetans who talk to foreigners, and we must be very careful. For the truth to get out to the world, some of us must leave Tibet as I have done. I ask you to be my spokespeople. Tell people about what I have told you. Please speak out for the freedom and rights of Tibetans.

Thank you for listening to my story. Truth is on our side because what I have told you is the truth. If you support the struggle for Tibetan freedom, you are working for the truth.

NAWANG CHOEDON

Born in Medrogonkar, Lhasa, Nawang Choedon comes from a farming background. Of ten children, she is the second oldest and as such was unable to go to school. Moreover, there was no proper school in the region. Her desire to study and get away from routine household affairs led her to become a nun in 1986. She participated in a series of demonstrations and was eventually arrested on 15th October 1989. After her release in 1992, she escaped to India. At present, she is at the Dolmaling Nunnery near Dharamsala.

WITH THE DECISION to become a nun, I went to the Tsam Kung Nunnery, which is near Lhasa. I was refused admission after I failed to clear the entrance test. I lived in Lhasa and learned from a tutor in the Nunnery. In the month of March 1988, there was a big demonstration for Tibet independence in the Barkhor area of Lhasa; I took part in it. During that demonstration, many of us escaped as thousands of people surrounded us to protect us from getting arrested. I had to return home for some time on the advice of my tutor. After spending three months at home, I was back in Lhasa. In the same month of the following year, I took part in another mass demonstration. In spite of strict vigilance by the Chinese authorities, I managed to escape. It was announced that persons without Themtho (registration card) must come to the police station for interrogation. I happened to be without Themtho at that time. I had to quickly send a message home asking them to bring my Themtho. I was in hiding until I got my Themtho. While I was in hiding at the Tsamkung Nunnery, a police official had visited my place and questioned the landlady about me. I once again left Lhasa to escape interrogation. After six months at home, I returned to Lhasa. I got admission into Chubsang nunnery near Sera Monastery. I had applied there after I failed to gain admittance at Tsamkung.

I was among the twenty Chubsang nuns leading the demonstration in front of Norbulingka on 2 September 1989 during the Shotun Festival. I escaped with the help of a Tibetan lady who acted as if she was my mother and that we had come to attend the festival. A month after that on October 15, 1989, we were only three nuns from Chubsang demonstrating in Barkhor. It had hardly been a few minutes since we started the protest march that a truck full of Chinese police came to arrest us. Each one of us had five to six Chinese police pouncing on us. I remember two police officials grabbing my hands, one official kicking me from the back and another one hitting me in front and kicking me in the stomach. Two police officials threw me into a police vehicle.

We were driven to the nearest police station in Lhasa. After reaching the police station, each one of us was taken to a separate room for interrogation. I was taken to one room. As I entered, I saw three men in the room. One of them was an interpreter. Questions like: "Who are the other conspirators? Who is instigating you to demonstrate?" were repeatedly asked. Upon getting no response, they would hit me on the neck and chest with the butt of the gun. When I still did not respond, one of them pointed his gun on my forehead and threatened to shoot me. Surprisingly, I was not scared to die. I thought of all the brave Tibetans who have sacrificed their lives for Tibet.

Then we were put in a truck and taken to Gutsa and handed over to the person in charge. We had to go through the whole process of interrogation once again. It was again, done in separate rooms. I saw ropes, chains and electric instruments lying on a table nearby. I was first made to sit on a chair. While questioning, my hand was tied behind my back with a rope and the tied hand was tied with another rope and the end of that rope was tied to the iron ceiling. Two of the men pulled the rope from the other side till I was hanging in the air with my hands lifted up in the air. The pain in my arms was unbearable and I was soon rendered unconscious. When I regained consciousness, I was on the floor with my hands released. But I could not move my hands. My wrists were blue with the mark of the tied rope. I was not in a position to get up on my feet. Someone was kicking me from the back. I was hit all over my body with a thick chain. I did not have answers for any of their questions, which annoyed them more. One of them picked up the electrical instrument and poked me in the nape of the neck, on the breast and inside my mouth with it. The pain was so terrible that after a while, I did not feel as if my body belonged to me. I still did not feel like listening or answering any of their questions. I was stripped naked and once again the electric prod was poked all over the upper part of my body. I saw them laughing at me. I was made to stand still for three hours. If I moved slightly, I would be slapped and beaten. At around midnight, I was taken to my cell. I was not tortured physically after the first day. After two and a half years in Gutsa, I was transferred to Trisum Prison where I was imprisoned for six months. I was released from the prison in 1992.

DASANG

Dasang was born in 1975 at Nemo Village in Phenpo Lhundup Dzong, north of Lhasa. His mother, sister and himself cultivated a twelve MU (1 MU = 25 sq. meters) smallholding. However, due to a grain taxation system their yearly income is never enough to sustain their small family. This has forced Dasang's older sister to work as a construction laborer in Lhasa for six months of the year to supplement the family income from their land.

MY FATHER WAS a shepherd but he died when I was very young. My mother is a farmer; she grows wheat and barley on our twelve MU of land. Though my family had been well off before the Chinese invasion, we are now very poor.

The Chinese taxation system keeps the farmers in my village in a perpetual state of impoverishment. Every year we have to sell about eight hundred Gyama (1 Gyama = 500 grams) of wheat to the authorities at a minimal price of twelve Yuan per Khel (1 Khel = 12 kilograms). In the past we could sell both barley and wheat. But these days the authorities accept only wheat. Each year we have to transport these eight hundred Gyama of wheat to a place called Chanka Xiang. We have pay about three Mao per Gyama to transport these by truck. One member of the family has to personally submit the grain to the Xiang (township) office.

At the office there is a huge grain storage with an opening in the roof through which the grain is poured after being measured. Usually the wheat is ground into flour and distributed among the Chinese officials in the area. It is also transported to China whenever there is some agricultural calamity.

Sometimes it is very difficult to produce the required quantity of wheat. Every year some officials come to the farm just before harvest time and fix the exact amount of Lhag Pu-Tsong (surplus grain sale) for each family. If the harvest turns out to be poor and we cannot produce the required quantity of wheat we have to compensate for the shortfall in cash.

To farmers this means a double burden: first we do not get the profit, which we would if we sold the grain in the open market; secondly we have to make up for any shortfall in the compulsory sale in cash. This happened twice in the last few years when the harvests were spoiled by heavy hailstorms.

If all goes well, my family has about 850 Gyama of barley or wheat left for our own consumption. We cannot sell this barley or wheat in this market, as we need all of it for our own consumption and as sowing for the next season. The Dzong (district) office does not give us any seeds.

Our yearly income is never enough to provide for the family. My older sister therefore works as a construction laborer in Lhasa for six months a year (three months in the winter and three months in the summer). Her wage supplements the income from the farm. The reason why she works in Lhasa rather than Phenpo is that there is not much construction work in our area. Even when there is some construction work it is usually Chinese who are employed. My sister earns three to four Yuan per day, depending on whether she knows the leader of the work unit or not. To earn this she works from morning until late afternoon with a lunch break of an hour-and-a-half.

* * *

There were not too many Chinese officials in Dasang's village. All officials were Tibetan. The top official was called

Buchung. He was a good man who did a lot of good work for the local Tibetans. He played a key role in the reconstruction of Dasang monastery in Nemo, 1985.

As far as Dasang knows, there were no foreign delegations in Nemo. When foreigners came to Lhundop dzong they were always taken to the only monastery which had been reconstructed with government funds. This monastery was in Gyaltong. All the other monasteries and nunneries in Lhundup dzong were reconstructed with money from the local population.

When Dasang was seventeen years old, he joined the monastery in his village. The main reason that he wanted to join a monastery was that he wanted to become educated. When he asked for admission at the monastery he was told that he had to go to the Choetsog in Lhasa to ask for permission. He did not go there, however, but went to Buchung instead. Buchung helped him to get admission in Nemo gonpa. Actually the maximum number of monks at this monastery was fixed at twenty-five. Dasang and four others were admitted as five official monks. They did not have to sign any official documents. Actually Dasang was very disappointed with the amount of education he received. There was no teacher or abbot. The three eldest monks (all twenty-five years old) took the responsibility of teaching the younger monks. There were many very young monks at the monastery. The youngest was only seven years old. Every year all thirty monks went around the village to collect donations for the monastery. If they did not get enough in their own village, they would go to other villages as well.

The donations were by far and large not enough to live on and the monks relied heavily on their families to provide them with food and basic necessities.

There was little political re-education at the monastery.

Once a year there was a general assembly with all the villagers, during which officials gave speeches about socialism etc. The monks from Nemo monastery never went to these meetings. Occasionally there would be a special political meeting for monks from the area. X, one of the oldest monks at the monastery, was supposed to go to these meetings which were held at the Gyaltog monastery. In reality, X did not go to these meetings. He just pretended to go, in order not to get into trouble with Buchung. There was hardly any checking at the monastery, which made it very easy to avoid these political meetings. Sometimes the authorities sent some booklets about socialism to the monastery. None of the monks ever read these booklets and would sometimes burn them.

The attitude of the authorities towards the attendance of monks at political meetings was rather indifferent; some years ago some monks made fun of a big political meeting where villagers from the whole dzong came together. After this incident the authorities did not put too much pressure on the monks to attend these meetings. Dasang suspects they might have been afraid that the monks would create trouble and chose to avoid such embarrassment.

Dasang did not know much about the history of Tibet before he came to the monastery. The monks did not talk much about politics, except for X. He gave Dasang some pamphlets and a speech of His Holiness' to read. After Dasang had read these texts and discussed them with X he tried to encourage some monks to come with him to Lhasa to demonstrate. He did not get much response however. X was afraid to go as he had been in prison before and thought it might be very bad for him to be arrested a second time. (X had been imprisoned for six months in 1987 for putting a flag on top of the Potala. When he was released from prison he could go back to the monastery, because he was not officially registered at Nemo monastery.)

In the village nobody talked about politics. Only a few older monks who did not stay in the monastery talked to Dasang about Tibetan history and the situation before 1959. Finally Dasang found a village boy called Migmar who was willing to help him put up some posters during a religious festival in Gyaldong monastery. On the 15th of the fourth Tibetan month Dasang and Migmar cycled to Gyaldong very early in the morning. They were carrying some posters that they had written the night before. The text on these posters were quotes from the pamphlets which Dasang had received from X. Actually they had been at a loss as to what to write on the posters, until X suggested to them they could copy his material. They also drew a Tibetan flag on a piece of paper and took it with them. It was about a four-hour drive to Gyaldang. When they arrived it was dawn. Very soon after they had put the posters and the drawing of the Tibetan flag on a wall outside the monastery people started collecting at the spot to read them. Those who could read told those who couldn that it was written well. People seemed to be very happy to see the posters. After some time the police came and took the posters off the wall. They took the posters with them to the Lhundup dzong police station. The police didn't come to the festival because they had been warned about the posters.

In the evening Dasang and Migmar went back to their village. After twenty days eight policemen (seven Tibetan and one Chinese) came to the monastery. They had his name and the name of the book from which he had copied some sentences on his poster. Dasang didn't know how they got his name. Perhaps some Tibetans had seen him when he and Migmar were putting up the posters. Perhaps some locals had pointed him out. Many locals knew him as he often went around the fields telling the farmers what he had heard on the radio from Voice of America.

The police searched his room and found a paper on which he had drawn the Tibetan flag. They took the flag and all his pens and asked him: "Where did you get the book from which you quoted?" He answered that the book was his. Then the police told him to gather his blankets and his thugpa bowl. They handcuffed him and took him to their car. The Chinese policemen held a revolver to his temple. It was quite a long walk to the car.

On the way Dasang's mother came up to them and held him very tightly. She pleaded with the police to release him, but they simply dragged him away. Dasang's mother followed them all the way to the car. Then she fainted and fell to the ground.

It was around lunchtime. Many laborers were on the way home. When they noticed Dasang surrounded by the police they came to the car. They blocked the road and shouted: "Why are you taking this boy along? He has not stolen anything! He has not killed anybody! Let him go!" Dasang estimates that there were about three hundred construction laborers who surrounded every policeman. The police couldn't move anywhere. They did not immediately start shooting at the crowd. Some local Tibetans came to the car and opened the door for Dasang. Dasang ran back to the monastery with his handcuffs still on. Other Tibetans started throwing stones at the car. The front window broke. Then two policemen, a Chinese and a Tibetan, started shooting at the crowd. At first they shot in the air. Then they started aiming at the crowd, which had already started to withdraw. Fortunately nobody was hit. Dasang reached the monastery safely. After some time, one of the policemen came up to the monastery with the key to his handcuffs. The policeman, who was Tibetan, unlocked his cuffs and told him: "This time we won't take you. But wherever you go, we will catch you." Later Dasang heard that the Tibetan laborers had told the police that they would kill them if they did not unlock Dasang's handcuffs.

One day later the police came back to the village to arrest Migmar. However, he got away in the same way.

During Dasang's escape from the car to the monastery three people were arrested. A monk named Dundup Gyalpo had been the first one to come forward to ask why the police took Dasang with them. He was beaten and in turn he threw some stones. Right now Dundup Gyalpo is in Sangyip prison. Dasang heard this from Y in Lhasa. Dhundup Gyalpo is seventeen years old. He is from the same village and the same monastery as Dasang. He was sentenced to three years imprisonment but committed suicide by jumping into the Trangpo River.

Two lay persons were arrested as well. Tsenang was the first among the local Tibetans to hit one of the policemen. He is thirty-two years old and the father of three children. Presently he is in Sangyip Prison serving a three-year sentence. Nyima Dundup was the second lay participant who was arrested. He is also from Nemo village. He is a nineteen-year old farmer, and was also sentenced to three years in Sangyip Prison. All three were arrested on the seventh day of the fifth Tibetan month.

On the evening of the seventh day of the fifth Tibetan month Dasang started to walk to Lhasa. When he arrived in Lhasa he stayed with X for one night. He told X what had happened to him and about the arrest of the three men. (Later X went to Phenpo to make inquiries about the three people. He gathered from their relatives that they were kept in Sangyip Prison.) Dasang tried to escape to India on the following day with a group of twenty-seven people. None of them had any documents. The police stopped them at Shigatse. Their luggage was searched. When the police found letters addressed to their relatives in India they were asked where they were going. They replied that they were on their way to Shakya on a pilgrimage. The police told them to go there and followed them with three police jeeps all the way to Shakya. After visiting Shakya they had no choice but to return to Lhasa. During the hassle with the police nobody was seriously hurt. Some people were slapped on the face when the police searched their luggage.

When Dasang reached Lhasa he decided not to go to his relatives, as the police might look for him there. He went to friends in Chusur and stayed in their house for a few months. He stayed inside the entire time, being afraid that the police might spot him outside. He spent most of his time reading religious texts. From his friends he heard that the police had indeed gone to his relatives in Lhasa to look for him. Dasang's friends contacted a guide who could take Dasang across the border. They paid the guide five hundred Yuan. On the evening of the twenty-fifth of the tenth Tibetan month, Dasang left Tibet in a truck. The next morning he arrived in Shigatse. Dasang and twenty-one other pilgrims spent the day in Shigatse visiting the Tashilungpo and buying some things in the market. In the evening the truck left for Tingri. It passed Tingri without any problems and let out the pilgrims. They walked for twenty-five days to Kodari. From there they took a bus to Kathmandu. They didn't get very far when the bus was stopped and seven policemen searched them. All twenty-two pilgrims were taken to a small dark room close to the market place in Kodari. All their new clothes, rings and other valuables were taken away. They had to hand over their shoes, instead of which they were given rubber slippers. They were not beaten, but the policemen threatened them: "If you don't give us what we ask, we'll send you to prison. Two of the policemen wore a uniform and the others didn't. They stayed in the small bamboo house for one day. On the market side on the house there was a small liquor store. Before they were let out, the police told them: "If you give us more money we'll arrange transport for you to Kathmandu. However, few of them had any money so they started walking to Kathmandu until a Tibetan bus driver who offered to take them to Kathmandu picked them up. Once the bus was stopped, the driver told Nepalese police they were pilgrims on their way to Kathmandu. He did not mention they were going to India. They reached Kathmandu without any more hassles.

Dasang stayed in the reception center for two weeks and reached Delhi on January 12, 1993.

Special Section: *Memories of Old Tibet*

About Ngodup Paljor—

These are the poems of a secretary to mountains, the poems of a man who walked mountains and crossed vast cultural divides more precipitous then grand canyons, while maintaining his curiosity and delight in the process of transformation. He walked over a bridge from the highlands of Western Tibet to life in Alaska's largest city. Along the way he was a refugee, a monk and a student, was fluent in Tibetan, Hindi, Sanskrit, Pali, Thai, and English; served as a translator for His Holiness the Dalai Lama, co-authored books with sinoasiatic authority John Blofeld; was an assistant professor of Tibetan studies at the University of Hawaii, and a cook and a longshoreman in Anchorage. But his real love was to hike the ridges and trails of mountains, bathe in icy water and write poems while drinking Tibetan tea near noisy streams. He himself served as a bridge for others to cross by offering his deep understanding of Buddhist philosophy, not only in the Tibetan Mahayana form but also of the Hinayana and Zen schools, to his American friends. Although his modesty did not allow him to call himself a teacher, he was, none the less, a teacher to those who knew him. His greatest desire was to help the Tibetan people overcome their suffering under the illegal occupation of their country and the conditions of exile in India and Nepal. He founded The Alaska Tibet Committee and Khawachen Dharma Center to help promote knowledge about Tibet. His compassion extended to all peoples and all of nature's energies; plants, rocks, animals, earth, air, and waters.

He studied the traditions of the original inhabitants of Turtle Island and felt kinship with them. He was a citizen of Mother Earth.

Paljor died as a result of an accident at the Port of Anchorage, while working as a longshoreman, full moon, October 25, 1988. He was around forty years old. These poems are all that are left, treasure them.

—Denise Lassaw Paljor

Untitled 1

Seeing a mother with daughter
Going hand-in-hand,
Laughing heartily and singing joyfully,
Memories of my childhood
Arose in my mind:
Curcumambulating the *stupa*
With my grandmother,
Reciting the Sacred Mantra:
OM MANI PADME HUNG,
OM MANI PADME HUNG,
OM MANI PADME HUNG.

Untitled 2

Now the wish of a poor poet
Is fulfilled:
To retreat in the thick
Dense snow
And write simple poems.

Untitled 3

Some come to Alaska
To dig the frozen tundra.
And others to hibernate
In igloos…
Well, comrades, to tell
You my reason,
Where else could a yak live,
Besides in wilderness and
Mountain

Untitled 4

Snow capped Mt. Denali
Frequently recalls reminiscences of my boyhood life:
Sleeping with a herd of yak
Drinking *Sho* (yogurt)
Eating *tsampa* (roasted barley flour)
Riding my favorite yak,
And rolling
down
    the
        lap
            of
                the
                    virgin
                        mountain.

Untitled 5

Lately my heart longs to see ravens.
I know they love to visit town in the winter.
And now snow is falling.
Yet, so far I have seen none.
Therefore, it hurts my heart.
They were my good friends when I was a little boy, and I miss them badly.
I used to know their language,
I would talk with them.
We called them Banchen, Great Messenger.

By chance, last year
I heard a raven singing.
Joyfully, I tried to understand him,
But I could not.

I know his song was very important.
So shock and disappointment
Filled my heart.

Right then, my mind flew
Back to my tiny village.
Poor and simple was our way of life;
Yet Banchen would come and sing for us.

Now, I don't see ravens much;
Even when I see them
I don't understand them.

It is indeed a sad thing,
Ah! it is indeed
Very sad.

Untitled 6

Wandering in the woods,
Inhaling the tranquility
Of nature,
My heart was stolen by an old
Fat tree.
There was something that
Pulled me to him,
Perhaps his nobility
And endurance,
To remain tranquil,
Despite his isolation
From his friends.

Untitled 7

When my bamboo flute sound was deep,
Birds of all feathers flocked around me
Without an invitation.

Now this broken flute shallow sound
Does not even draw the attention of sea gulls.

Untitled 8

Homer, the land gifted
With boundless natural beauty:
Above, the bright-smiled mountains,
Below, the cosmic dances of fish,
In the middle, gleeful songs of birds;
The land of tall trees
And healthy people.
Truly, nature is generous,
Nothing is missing here:
The trees for brushes,
The ocean my ink,
And the earth my paper.

Untitled 9

Mountains, why do you choose me
As your secretary?
Don't you know my
Spellings are poor
And handwriting
Is illegible?
Above all, do you
Think people of these
Days understand your words:

I know that your
Messages are immensely
Important.
But, my writing skill
Does not permit me to convey them.

Untitled 10

When my father left his body,
I inherited a wooden cup.
Some day when I die,
Do you know what I am going
To leave for my inheritance?
A cotton stuffed zafu.

Untitled 11

Denali, the mountain endowed
With beauty and charms,
The Queen of the mountains
In North America:
When I see your bright face,
I remember the smiling face
Of your sister
Joma Lungma, The Goddess of the
Earth.
I grew on her lap,
I played with her children.

Untitled 12

The wish of my Amala
Was for me to become
A Buddhist monk,
Dedicating my life to follow
The footsteps of the Lord Buddha:
But her wish was disappointed.

The wish of my father
Was for me to succeed as
A man of high degree,
Earning my life working
For the government of Tibet;
Yet, his wish too, was unfulfilled.

Now, neither a monk
Nor a man of high degree,
I have no specific wish to pursue
Nor am I giving up to have a wish.
Generally, I follow the way of the clouds,
I eat when I am hungry,
And I drink when I am thirsty.

A MEMORY OF MY CHILDHOOD IN TIBET

By Ngodup Paljor
Edited by Denise Lassaw Paljor

TO THE OUTSIDER Tibet has always been the Land of Magics and Mysteries, the deadly forbidden country. But to the inhabitants it has always been a land of religion, in Tibetan *CHO DEN GYAL KHAB*, and, it is our beloved home.

My home town, Zonga, belongs to the Central U Tsang province though it is on the far edge of the province, a few days from Mount Kailash. Literally Zonga means Happy Fort or Castle, it is situated in between two rivers. Zonga has an unimaginable landscape. Surrounded by huge mountain ranges, always capped with snow, fantastic forms of gorges, rocks, precipices and streams. It is an open life in Zonga where people seek simplicity, solitude, the feel of the weather, and live in close acquaintance with animals. Mountain goats, antelopes, deer and other wild animals wander freely as in primitive days. A day without seeing wild animals and hearing the beautiful song of birds would be unthinkable.

The density of population in Zonga was pretty thick compared to many villages and towns in Tibet. If my speculation is right there were four hundred mud-brick houses in Zonga and a beautiful Gompa (monastery) in the heart of the village. Zonga was divided in two parts, the Upper Zonga and the lower Zonga of which my family belonged to Upper Zonga.

75

There was a strong spirit of competition between the children of the two factions of Zonga and often bloody clashes and fighting occurred. Many times the elders helped stop the fighting and cautioned with threatening words of warning whenever the children gathered to play. I was a pretty tough boy but I would never go to lower Zonga without someone to accompany me.

Generally people in Zonga are farmers. We grew barley, wheat, buckwheat, potatoes, turnips, onions, beans and radish, but we also have to raise animals and other sources of provisions. Some of my uncles were nomads. They used to take care of animals and bring us dairy products such as cheese, butter and meat and in exchange we would give them cereals such as barley, wheat and beans.

Twice a year there is a big gathering of traders from all walks of life in Zonga. Since Zonga is very close to Nepal the merchants from Mustang would also come during such a congregation of the traders. As there was no market or shop in my town, so it was a great spectacle for all of the children and adults to watch the transactions of goods and the gathering of the traders. I used to insist that my father let me go with him, and I wanted to help with whatever I could. I very seldom saw my father giving currencies, most business were done through the barter system. Several times my father had to haggle and bargain since there were no fixed prices and often it was hard to know the value of the new goods imported from Nepal and India.

Most of the traders were nomads and they would spend some days visiting their friends and relatives when the business was over. In Tibet, generally the nomads are well known for their honesty and simplicity. Tibetans call them by the nickname of Akudropa (Uncle Nomad). At one time we had a nomad guest who had never tasted molasses. He got seriously sick for several months due to over consumption of molasses and it took a very long time to recover from the sickness. I was told by my mother that he later decided not ever to touch molasses. Perhaps it was my mother most favorite story whenever I asked her for molasses.

The way of life goes with the nature in Tibet. In spring the nature begins to come up like a little baby. One can see small plants and grass appear after several months buried under the snows. For farmers it is a time for plowing and sowing. I would never forget this season because the first day of plowing begins with a colorful celebration. Farmers decorate their oxen with new earrings and bells and give them delicacies and *chang*, beer made from barley. On such a day my uncles and other relatives would come to help us. The first day of plowing means only celebration. It is a day of great fun and joy. Everybody would come in their best dresses and spend the whole day drinking and eating. For me the most exciting part of the ceremony was to see animals gaily decorated with earrings and bells and to feed them with delicacies. As the bell and scepter are for a Vajrayana lama, so is the land to farmers. There is a lot of rituals and tradition with respect to handling the land. The farmers call their land fortune, to them it means everything. One thing I can still remember is that the land is never to be divided into two. If it happens that the time comes for splitting one land into two, then it is a bad omen which means splitting is happening in the family.

While myself and my brother were kids of seven and nine years old, our parents would tell us that my brother should take care of the land and family properties. Of course when Ngodup (my first name) enters the Gompa he has no right to any worldly possessions such as land, yet as you are a layman it is your responsibility to serve him and give everything that comes from the field that the families has given for him. It is a sinful karma if Ngodup simply eats the monastery food and doesn't practice dharma, then he will be born in a lower rebirth such as animals and so forth. He spoke these words very clearly and so many times so that we could remember our duties and obligations.

My work before I entered the monastery was to collect yak dung or horse dung for our family cooking fire. Sometimes I had to go to look after the cattle when we sent out our cattle to join the village herd. One boy or girl from four houses takes turns to look after the village herd. I was always eager to go when my family turn came. One of the most pleasant memories of going there was to share the food prepared from one's own house. We set cattle to graze on the meadows and we played and listened to the stories about wolves and shepherds. Sometimes we used to run races with little calves. The whole day was very pleasant and carefree. Unlike other times there was no fear of a coming attack from the wolf nor feeling of loneliness.

The most happy and favorite season for all Tibetans is the summer. The hills are full of berries and everywhere you can see green grass and a variety of flowers. It is the season for picnics, recreations as well as religious festivals. During this time the youngsters would spend their summer in merry making while the older would go to the temples and busy themselves merit making. Like most Tibetans the people of Zonga are very pious and devoted in the religious observances.

They offer donations to the temple and give alms to the beggars. Besides the observances in the monastery there is a lot of other religious events outside the monastery. I remember very vividly that I used to go with my grandmother to listen to the Mani lama (Dharma story teller). The storyteller brings a thanka (a scroll painting) depicting the story of the Buddha or Boddhisattvas. He blows a conch shell three or more times so as to make an announcement of his presence and calling for all the dharma practitioners to come to listen to the noble life story of the Buddha or Bodhisattva as the day being very auspicious to accumulate the merits. He narrates the story with a melodious tune and a good sense of humor. The listeners bring some grain or anything as an offering and sit listening to the story as long as they want to. I had seen several times with my grandmother and others shedding tears. I didn't understand at that time the reason of her shedding tears. Now as I give more thought on the contents of the stories which were about the lives of the Buddha and Boddhisattva who have gone through accumulating a stock of merits and sat countless years in Samadhi for the attainment of buddhahood for the benefit of all sentient beings, I couldn't help but cry and shed tears also.

For a true and devout Buddhist woman like my grandmother it is not a matter of wonderment when she sheds tears while listening to the Dharma story. The stories are very moving and full of wonderful teachings which strengthen and bestow a strong inspiration to continue the Dharma practices, which to Tibetans means everything in one's life. As a child of seven years there was not much fun listening to the stories but illustrations of the stories were very thrilling and fascinating to look at. My grandmother pointed to the pictures of hell beings and warned me that I should refrain from killing any being else I might be born in such an undesirable realm. Since then I was reluctant to harm any being. I guess it was merit of going with my grandmother that I had acquired much feeling of compassion to all beings.

At one time I and Nima (my younger sister) were left alone at home while our parents had left for a day to pay respect to the shrine. It was a day journey from Zonga. At first we didn't realize that we were left alone as we were in deep sleep. We woke up and called mother but she was not at home. Our house seemed very quiet and empty, even our watchdog seemed in a silent retreat. I jumped out of the bed, and ran to find our parents but nobody was at home. All I found were good bread, dry meat and some cheese that our mother had left for us. I woke up Nima and told her that all were gone some where else. She began crying and started calling mother. I tried hard to keep her calm and finally after hours of crying she came near to me. We played together rolling the big round bread. We ate half of it and the rest we gave to our dog. The day was very long. We felt very empty, missing our parents. Still the memory of that day is very fresh in my mind. From this experience I can say that for a child, mother means everything. Losing mother means losing everything. In the evening we heard the voices of our parents coming. We dashed to see mother and we hugged her breast and requested her many times not to leave us alone. She was deeply touched by our request and from then onwards she never left us alone without someone to look after us.

In the mid-summer, monks and lay people go round the field. They carry sacred scriptures, images, and other religious objects. Some carry prayer flags, umbrellas, banners, and other religious articles. It is a colorful and pompous festival. Everyone wears their gala dresses. The monks say prayers and blow conches and trumpets. The lay people burn incense and sing the songs of joy and fun. One farmer says at the top of his voice, let there be rain and let there be blessing, then everybody repeats after him. The smoke of incense fills the air. In the evening the people gathered at the courtyard of the monastery for folk dance and drinks where there is plenty of *chang* prepared for the dancers and singers by the community. Older people and kids watch the dances while young people take part in the dance. For me it was very exciting and fascinating to see my mother, sisters and an aunt who was a very good dancer and singer as well.

The end of summer means beginning of a lot of work for people from all walks of life in Tibet. Everyone gets a vivid hint of the coming fall by noticing the changes take place in the nature. It is a period of coming decay and fading away of the lovely and beautiful flowers and small plants. Leaves start falling off and meadows turn a yellowish color. For Chopas (religious practicioners) it is a good reminder of impermanence, everything changes and passes away from moment to moment. Thus it rejuvenates the teachings of transitoriness and bestows a strong inspiration to lead their lives according to religious discipline. But for farmers it is an indication that it is time to get ready for harvesting and preparing for the cold and weird winter life. During time of harvest we set up tents near the fields and sleep in the open space. Chilly winds disturbs sleep from time to time, yet openness and watching a thousand stars are such amazing euphoria. I still recollect the memories of those days.

The most bothering for kids during this time of camping out in the open air is to go out for a piss. As the weather is cold I had to go many times in the night. I was always afraid of the Yidak, hungry ghosts. There are so many stories and legends about spirits and ghosts who take the human beings in the night. It is believed that when someone calls less than three times then it is the spirit who is calling. Therefore one should always call more than three times to the waiting person or make a visit to him. On dark new moon nights I dared not go alone whenever I had to go for a piss. I needed someone to accompany me. Most of the time my father accompanied me and often he taught me the names of stars, galaxies, and constellations.

What he had taught me were out of my memory now but I remember one thing from our legends, he said, the eagle and the dragon go as a sling. He pointed out the stars of the Seven Sisters of the North and other stars. Watching thousands of stars was so fascinating and euphoric that I always felt that those were the abodes of the buddhas.

During harvesting I loved playing with straw that had been cut, making a little house and hiding among the straw was one of the most favorite games. There were no toys of any kind in my village, so we played with whatever we could find in the nature. Sons of both rich and poor play with the mud, grass, flowers and stones. In the winter we sat on flat stones and slid on the frozen streams. Tugging, rolling, wrestling, and riding on the animals were the games of my childhood in Tibet. Whistling and singing while working is part of the inborn character of the Tibetan people.

At the nighttime the farmers gather in tents. Soon after the dinner is over, the workers begin to sing and drink *chang*. It is time for rest and relaxation. Those who have completely exhausted their energies may go to bed right after dinner, but many of them stay for drink. As everyone gathers round for drink and social gatherings, it is the most pleasant part of harvesting time. Sometimes the stories of Aku Tompa, the legendary rascal of Tibet, are told. His stories are full of jokes, tricks, deceptions, and stealings. Tibetans believe that Aku Tompa was an emanation of the Lord Chenrezig who had appeared in Tibet to teach the arts of tricks. Jokes, songs and hearty laughters keep everyone awake and alert until very late in the night. Almost every night there is a singing competition. Some may sing songs composed by themselves while others sing songs from the past. Some people sing the songs written by

Tseyang Gyaltso, the Sixth Dalai Lama. His poetry and love-song are the favorite for all Tibetans. Here I quote some of his songs:

This girl was perhaps not born from a mother, but blossomed in a peach tree...
Her love fades more quickly than a peach flower.

*

If a maidens love is undying
My chang will remain everlasting
The eternal refuge of this young man
Must be indeed to put trust in these

*

Although I know her soft body
I cannot comprehend her mind,
Yet, by making a mere drawing on the ground
The distance of the stars in the sky
Can be calculated!

To the minds of many Westerners the people of the Buddhist faith are pessimistic by nature. Life is full of suffering and miseries. Some of them seem to believe the Buddhists even have no sense of humor or laughters in their daily life. I admit that Buddhism teaches that life is lousy and not a bed of roses. But it is so amazing the Buddhists do not seem to be bothered or affected by the pessimistic teachings. I have seen the Buddhists of my own country, and countries like Burma, Thailand, and Laos who are perhaps the most happy people in the present world. They are generous, carefree, easy-going but true seekers of the truth and they have plenty of leisure time to talk and play dice and dominos. Tibetans love enjoying their life to live in warmth and comfort, yet they pay their fullest attention to make good use of their precious human body. Daljor gi mi lus Rimpoche, is the path of the Buddha teachings so they can be freed from the Samsara and thus help other beings to gain the same stage. This popular expression may throw some light on the Tibetan philosophy of life. When you are in the Dharma Hall you should practice the dharma. When you are in the Dance Hall you should take part in the dance.

In Tibet the prospects of a child's life are chosen by their parents. My parents decided to make me a monk from birth because they already had my elder brother who was going to take care of family business. Matters of my ordination were frequently discussed among the relatives when I reached the age of seven and a half. I was told the prospects of my future career as a monk and the advantages of monastic training. I was eager to enter the Gompa and become a learned monk. My parents had a number of good reasons. In my village it is an aged tradition that the second son should enter into the Gompa, naturally they made that decision to make me a monk so as to keep the tradition. Other reasons were that I could receive a good education and could earn a high honor and respects from the general public if I became a learned monk. Also there are many occasions when the lay man needs the monk's help, such as to recite the sacred sutras in the time of the relative's death or sickness and to give teachings when the relatives are heavily depressed by the ups and downs of family affairs. Tibetans believe that to make a child a monk can earn an enormous stock of merit.

Having consulted for the most auspicious day for entering into the monastery I was ordained as a novice on the birthday of the Lord Buddha. I was very happy and excited for a couple of weeks for I seemed to be the main figure of attention and attraction. My parents and relatives offered me gifts and Katak (white scarves) as a token of their warmest compliments. There was no work to do, no looking after the animals, no pressures from parents.

My lama who was my uncle seemed very kind and gentle. I began to feel that this must be Dewachen, the land of bliss, which I had heard of from my grandmother. But soon my lama's facial expression began to change and he assigned me a lot of daily chores. To get up early in the morning which I hated most, to sweep the floor, light the votive butter lamps and make water offerings to the Buddha . He reminded me several times about my new life as a novice and admonished me thus, "Ngodup, now you are not the same as you were at home. Now you are in the Gompa and you are a novice, therefore you should be clean and neat and never do such acts that make lay people unhappy or have unpleasant feelings." I responded him that I would do my best although I didn't understand what are the acts that will make people happy. He explained the manners and ethics of the novice and the proper ways to make offerings to the Triple Gem.

After a month I joined the Chostra (dharma class) with other young novices. There were two sessions a day, one in the morning and one in the evening. Primary lessons were reading script and a lot of memorization of the scripture texts. As time went by I made good progress in my studies and my lama gave me some lenience to visit my parents and relatives. I was remarkably impressed by the respect and appreciation my parents and relatives showed for my way of life. Their cares and concerns made me very happy and it further strengthened my will to continue my life in the Gonpa.

One of the horrible experiences in the monastery was the strict disciplines and hardships that I had to go through. All other disciplines didn't bother me much but to get up early in the morning particularly in the winter time was the most terrible experience that I can imagine. So much so that once I ran away from the monastery to my aunt's house. I knew my lama would go directly to my parent's house so that would not be the right place for refuge. I requested my aunt not to tell anybody and spent two days at my aunt's house. On the third day she took me back to the monastery and made an earnest request to my lama not to punish me for the offense of running away. She in fact did confess that it was her fault. I used to go to see her every time when I got into troubles. She loved me dearly as her own son. My lama gave me excuses this time for it was the first time that I had left the monastery without his permission. But he warned me that he would not be a compassionate lama if I ever did it again. The days that I spent together with my aunt were unforgettable in my life. She was a kind and tenderhearted young woman, and the cares and love that she gave me were more than any other relative. I miss her so much and I have no doubt that she must be missing me too. It has been almost twenty years that we haven't had any contact with each other. A long separation has kept us completely ignorant about our lives. She would have escaped out of Tibet if she wanted to but she remained in her strong conviction to live in Zonga so long as her aged mother continued to live. No matter what might happen to her she was willing to go through it. All her brothers and sister left the house yet she remained faithful and took care of her mother. I have no way to know how she is doing in Tibet. All that I can say is my prayer for her long life and wish that we can meet each other before our departure from this planet. It seems a long way to accomplish this dream but who knows what will happen in the next year. Everything changes. Today the sky is cloudy yet same things won't be tomorrow.

The most happy time in the monastery was the New Years time. For a couple of weeks you can do a lot of things. Rules are very relaxed except if you violate some major precepts, that deprive the validity of the monkhood. Monks have a great role to perform the ceremonial rites and rituals for the auspiciousness of the coming New Year. Besides this the monks perform Dharma dances on the eve of New Year. Lay devotees come to make offerings to the monks and together celebrate the New Year with much joy and leisure. I loved the New Year day as it provided me with time to play with other kids in the street and I could sleep either at home or in the monastery. There were many good foods of all kinds and plenty of time to play in the streets without fear of punishment for roaming. Laymen and monks played dice, cards and dominos at the same table. In preparation for New Years oranges and apples were brought from Nepal and stored in a room with an iron gate in the monastery. I sharpened a long stick and stuck the oranges and ate them with another young novice. No one caught us.

I guess the New Year means a lot to everyone and it is the day every kid dreams about all the time, especially the young novice of my age in Tibet. There are no other long holidays or vacations in the monastery. The other times of the year life is very strict. Hardship and strict disciplines are designed for the purification of the karmic deeds that one might have committed in the past. Punishments from the lamas should be honored as a token of blessings rather than other negative feelings. Such were the days when I was in the monastery.

I don't remember much of my monastic life in Tibet. I was in the monastery for one and a half years. Memories of my childhood in Tibet are jumbled because of so many places and countries that I had to go through. Not because of my own will, but the wild wind of karma that blew me here and there. Reflecting on it now I have missed some parts of my childhood by living away from my parents and brothers and sisters. I didn't get much time to play with them. However, I am always grateful to my parents who have done their best to make my life the most meaningful and the best suited to our traditions in those days.

I now realize the role monasteries play in shaping and educating the people and their way of life. Homesickness and missing sisters and aunts were the worthwhile struggles and hardships that I had to go through. I have no complaints to anybody who punished me for breaking rules of the novice. At least they did it to make me perfect and to benefit for my life. Life in the monastery wasn't that hard once you got used to the self-discipline. One of my lamas asked me, "What do you think, Thubten Sherab (my novice name) layman life or monk's life? Which do you think the more pleasant thing?" I responded to him the layman life, whereupon he told me, well you think the layman life is easier than the monks? Don't you think that to carry a hundred sacs of grain is more difficult that to recite one hundred Tara mantra?

Editor's note:

When the Chinese came to Zonga they gave everyone silver money in exchange for the Tibetan Sang notes but soon this was replaced with foreign paper money of no real value. Then they began to take young children away from the parents and send them to be educated in China. Paljor's parents were very much against this and their views were known. One night a neighbor came to their house and warned them that they would be the subject of the next days *thamzing* or group struggle sessions where the accused were supposed to admit and repent of their wrong views. These session often ended with the accused badly beaten or even killed. To not participate in the sessions was to be sure to be the next subject. So in the night Paljor parents gathered up their children, Chophel, Pajlor, Lhakpa, Nima, and Dodup and ran for the borderlands of Mustang. They hid the children with their nomad relatives and went back to Zonga. They lived apart from the children for perhaps a year and finally things got so bad they escaped again and made their way down the trails of Mustang. Paljor told me stories of this terrible trip, how he saw an avalanche of rock sweep a group of Tibetans off a narrow trail and into the deep canyon; how his grandmother bravely jumped into a rushing icy river to save a woman who had fallen in, only to be swept away in the current. They never found her. Though he was usually hungry himself when he met a sick man along the trail he gave him his bread. When the family reached Kathmandu there were already people helping the flood of Tibetan refugees. Their helper gave them their train tickets to India and told him they could get on the train. "Where is the train?" Paljor's father asked.

"Right there." The helper pointed.

"That's the train?" We thought it was a strange house on wheels! In India Paljor's family's story mirrors the stories of thousands of other refugees, but that Paljor was able to continue his education at foreign universities and become the first Tibetan to settle in Alaska, makes his story unique.

-- Denise Lassaw Paljor

TASHI PALDEN

Tashi Paldon was interviewed in 2000 at her home in Salt Lake City.

Please state your name, age, birthplace, and current home.

My name is Tashi Palden, and I am 55. I was born in Lhasa, and came to America in 1987. I now live in Salt Lake City, Utah.

How long did you live in Tibet?

I lived mainly in Lhasa until 1985, when I fled to India.

Why did you leave?

Living in Lhasa was very unbearable due to very poor conditions. The Dalai Lama was in India. In Tibet, in general, every aspect was poor. Tibetans do what the Chinese say. They [the Chinese] are destroying the culture and exploiting the resources.

Describe your family situation. What was childhood like? What did you do?

When I was younger, the conditions my family lived in weren't very good, but still better than under the Chinese. Tibetans were free to do whatever they wanted. My father worked for the Tibetan government and my mother was a housewife. I had one brother and four sisters.

Why were you imprisoned?

Since the Chinese occupation, Tibetans did not want to stay under the Chinese rule. Tibetans have had uprisings since then. During the Cultural Revolution, all of the provinces had uprisings, and I was caught in it. I was in my mid-twenties at this time. My younger brother was in a Chinese school in Tibet, and he was a member of a [Tibetan] revolutionary party in high school. During that time, if a son was involved in revolutionary activities, the Chinese would go after the whole family. My brother did not want to endanger the family so he did not live with us. My mother was sick and had heart problems and did not want him to leave because he was the only son. Knowing she was not going to live long, she put me in charge of taking him to India. I prepared everything for my brother's escape, but as we reached the border in Dhingri, we were all caught. We had to lie to the Chinese government, saying that we were meeting relatives. That was the last day I saw him.

After the Chinese caught him, he was put in prison for being a revolutionary and for being a follower of the Dalai Lama and the Panchen Lama. I was imprisoned for encouraging my brother to follow the Dalai Lama and the Panchen Lama. I was there for fifteen years. At first I was in the Sanghi prison, and then I was moved to Drapchi prison.

What happened after you left the prison?

My father was still in prison, having been sentenced to twenty years for being in the old Tibetan goverment. When I left Lhasa a few months later to go to India, people would ask me about Lhasa, but I could not really answer.

What had changed in the fifteen years you spent in prison?

There was drastic change. When I first went into prison, you could see a lot of Tibetans. But after fifteen years all of the temples and monasteries were destroyed. To visit the hospital you needed a certificate of sickness. Everything looked Chinese. I was kind of lost in the streets. There were new houses in front of the Sera monastery. And behind it were all of the broken statues and ruins—covered by tarps.

Describe the prison and your experiences there.

When I first went into prison in 1969, other prisoners said that the prison conditions were a little bit better than they had been ten years earlier. I didn't get much food, but the men were even more underfed. I was fed three times a day, just *tsampa* and black tea. Prisoners I talked to who were in the prison earlier said that they would fight over mice and leftovers. Sometimes they would eat human feces. It was said that Chinese excrement was worse than Tibetan excrement. Every day we would go outside and build things. The men would break the rocks and the women would carry the rocks. Sometimes people would eat the human flesh dropped by vultures overhead from a Tibetan burial.

One month in the year we did not have to do any hard labor. Instead we were asked about our feelings towards the Chinese—this was called education. We were given a few documents that would say good things about China and bad things about other countries—international studies. We had to denounce our former actions to our cellmates and accept the Chinese way. "China is the best, America is the worst," was commonly taught. They told us that America was beautiful only in the papers, but in real life America, as well as India, should be considered evil. At the end of education month, they made us write a summary paper of the bad actions of these two countries [America and India]. They made us sign this paper.

I was considered a political prisoner, and was guarded more heavily than other prisoners. It was understood that when I was released, I would be labeled a black cap. This meant that when I was released, I would be labeled a black cap. This meant that the neighbors were supposed to watch me. As a political prisoner, I was not allowed to leave the prison. Despite the fact that other prisoners were allowed one visit per month, I wasn't allowed any at all.

Were you the subject of witness to any human rights violations/torture? Explain.

There was a meeting. They called all the prisoners together. We weren't allowed to look around or even look at each other. Whenever these meetings were called, we knew that someone would die. After we were marched out, we were surrounded by armed guards. Though we did not witness the execution, someone was always missing when we returned to our cells.

Prisoners weren't allowed to talk about the torture. I was never tortured, but I knew and heard of people who were. One lady was imprisoned for tearing down a poster of Mao. She was sentenced to seven years in prison for tearing down this poster. When her seven years were up, she was executed. This lady had been poor before she came to prison, even though the Chinese said they were taking care of the poor. The Chinese found a picture of His Holiness the Dalai Lama in her house and confiscated it. This upset her so greatly, so she tore the poster.

I would want people to picture this. Every morning when I woke up, I could hear the screams and cries of the men through the wall. The Chinese were very hard on them. They were put through torturous question and answer sessions. Sometimes the Chinese acted nice, but they were being two-faced, using emotional blackmail. They would ask questions like, "What about your future?" to make people do what they wanted them to do. They used every weapon. When my brother and his friends were publicly executed, for example, I was given a set of his clothes, torn and bloody.

Whenever foreigners visited, the guards made us change clothes and made sure we were clean. They tidied up the prison and changed everything, including the bed mattresses.

In Lhasa the torture was not as bad, not like in Kham and rural areas. Bamboo under the fingernails, tied up and questioned...but even in my prison people were treated so badly, they tried to commit suicide, but couldn't. One prisoner was beaten so bad, her kidneys were damaged. Other people received electric shocks and I saw cattle prods used as torture devices.

What was the hardest part of your ordeal?

The hardest day of my life was when my brother was executed by the Chinese.

What has improved since 1959?

I don't feel that the Chinese have NOT done any good. They have developed things, but not things that necessarily needed to be developed.

Tell us about your brother's execution.

I was there for my brother's execution. They tied me up so I couldn't see it, but I remember that the faces of my brother and his friends were unrecognizable because they were beaten so badly. Something was put in their mouths to prevent them from praising His Holiness.

All were teenagers. There was my brother and I think twelve others, between age sixteen and nineteen, and one was thirty. Their deaths were not in vain.

Each of their families had to pay for the second bullet (the government did the first for free). The families also had to pay for the rope. After the shootings, a hole was dug.

My sisters tried to recover my dead brother's body so that we could feed his body to the vultures, a traditional Tibetan burial. But they were beaten up for trying to dig up the body with their hands. The families of the executed were forced to come to a meeting, where they were to thank the officials for executing their sons.

If you could say one thing to the world, what would it be?

I am illiterate. When I was planning my brother's escape, I told him to tell others what is happening in Tibet. Support the truth, help Tibet.

ANI PACHEN

Fifty seven years old and an ex-guerilla fighter, Pachen Dolma was born in Gojo, Kham. Being the only child and with her family belonging to one of the nine chieftain households of the region, she was privately tutored. At an early age, she decided to renounce worldly affairs and become a nun.

ONE NIGHT IN 1950, a public meeting was held where all high lamas, government authorities and people gathered to discuss the imminent threat of Chinese attack on us. Plans and strategies were worked out to prevent Chinese invasion of our land. My father was one of the main leaders. We then started defending our borders and did not allow a single Chinese to live in Gojo. Many people lost their lives in the struggle. My father died of hypertension as he was very worried with the situation of the time. I took on his responsibility and became the Gojo chieftain. My father had taught me how to handle guns and other weapons at an early age.

The Chinese soldiers were advancing further into the region with every victory. My unit had retreated to Sershung. One day we were ambushed unexpectedly by the Chinese soldiers. Many people were killed. I, along with some of my unit, escaped to Sherta Lho and from there to Palbar. We stayed at Palbar for a month and during that time met some Tibetans who were being trained by Americans. We joined hands with them. Once again, the Chinese soldiers overpowered us and arrested all of us. I tried to escape with my people but we were arrested at Sherta Lho. At the time of my arrest, even my grandmother, mother, and aunt were arrested. We were detained in Rop.

Then there was interrogation. I was taken to a room alone for questioning. I was asked a whole lot of questions for which I had no answers. Getting no response, I was whacked with a cane stick, slapped in the face and kicked in the stomach. My whole face got swollen up with the beatings. The cane stick was also used to hit me on the body. I requested them to kill me as the pain was becoming too much. They tied both my hands together at the back with a rope. My hand was tied to another rope and on to the ceiling. I was hung in the air with my hands tied to a rope in the ceiling. After a few seconds, I fell unconscious. I regained consciousness only when someone sprinkled water on my face. I found myself on the floor with my hands untied. My hands were swollen and I could not move them at all. My eyes were swollen and bruised and my eyeballs felt as if they were going to come out. I had nothing to say.

Psychological pressure was exerted. Even worse than beating is the psychological pressure; you did this, and you did that, give away the names of other people, etc. It makes you so depressed, it almost drives one mad. It went on like this. They said our crimes would have to be confessed. I and Tamdin Choekey, in Chamdo prison, were shackled for over a year. During that time, we were struggled with, [and] I lost my hair. The same question was asked during two or three interrogation sessions a day.

We were told to confess our crimes We were asked what wealth we had, and if we fought in the rebellion against the Chinese, and how did the others fight, etc. Then accusing us of not confessing properly, they beat us, pulled out our hairs, beat our faces with sticks so hard that my eyeballs felt as if they were going to fall out. We were suspended upside-down from the ceiling and beaten with sticks.

If one was suspended like this for a long time, one would fall unconscious. As I fell unconscious, they would lower me on the ground and revive me with a splash of water. Then, I would be interrogated. Since I could not answer their questions, they would accuse me of not telling the truth and pull me in the air, once again. They did this to me many times, once every week or two.

I suffered enormously for want of adequate food, shelter, and clothes. When we were first imprisoned, we had only two meals a day. We were always hungry. In Chamdo, we were given about three teaspoons of barley flour in the morning, with a small can of black tea. The same amount of ration was given in the evening. There was no lunch, and no other food was provided for the prisoners. The clothes that we wore on the first day of our imprisonment were the same garments worn throughout the whole of the prison term, without change, night and day! So, our bodies were full of lice and nits. Nobody was allowed to go outside, even to ease oneself! During that time the Chinese did not give us any education. The only thing they repeatedly said was: "Think over yourself. If you bring change in yourself, then we will release you!" I had to stay in a dark cell. In that cell there was a tin for defecation, which was not cleaned for some twenty days. Insects buzzed about. One cannot tell if it is day or night in such conditions. Occasionally, when I was taken out in the light, I felt dizzy and saw red everywhere. I felt a pang of pain in my stomach, because there was no food in the stomach.

Some prisoners had their arms and legs shackled. I and Khando Chime Gonpo's wife, had our legs shackled. Khando Chime Gonpo was a renowned man. He was one of the ministers of Derge King. At that time, I was young. But she was about fifty. Her teeth had fallen out. We were shackled for more than a year. When we went to the toilet, we had to walk with the chain on our legs. Tibet, as you know, is a cold region. So, the iron shackles made us feel cold. Besides, there was no food in my stomach. I would fall unconscious from time to time. Some inmates told me that they felt tempted to eat their own feces. Such was the hunger in the prison.

Samye Monastery (an important monastery close to Lhasa), was also turned into a prison and some of the inmates there had to feed on animal hides. To stay alive, some of them felt so hungry when that when they went to the toilet, they ate human excrement. Deshong and Gashe Tsering Palmo had to eat human flesh when they were in Deyong prison. Both daughters of Derge Lingstang also had to feed on human flesh out of hunger, and later both of them died. Some of the Tibetan prisoners had to commit suicide by jumping into the river, as they could no longer tolerate the torture of the Chinese. Similar conditions prevailed throughout Tibet.

Thousands died of starvation, countless numbers of people committed suicide, and thousands died of Chinese torture and atrocities.

I was taken to Lhasa Drapchi prison which was the first prison in the whole of Tibet. I spent eleven years in that prison. There were more than two hundred women inmates when I was transferred there. Other than the two hundred women prisoners, there were lamas, *Tulkus* freedom fighters, aristocratic family members, and intellectuals.

While in Drapchi prison, I had to work with other prisoners from early in the morning, through the late night, with only one morsel of a meal at noon. We had to carry bricks on our backs like pack animals, and as a result wounds developed on our backs. Not only that, we had to clean the Chinese toilets with our bare hands! Geri Shak Ani, a nun who was one of the main activist during the Tibetan Women Uprising in Lhasa in 1959, was again tortured along with three women during the same period, when there was anti-Teng-Shao-Ping fever.

* * *

In terms of property destruction, the Chinese had destroyed thousands of monasteries in Tibet. All the invaluable images, statues, ritual instruments, and jewels, corals, and all the precious things were carried away to China. Buddhist scriptures were burned, and Mani stones (sacred objects) were used as slabs to build staircases, so that the people would tread upon them. The monks were ousted from the monasteries. The monasteries were reduced to ruins. There was not a single monastery that had its roof intact. The overwhelming destruction of property and the inhuman treatment of the people of Tibet by the Chinese invaders was not concentrated in one area. It happened in the whole of Tibet, including Derge, Ganze, and Lingkar Shepa since 1959 and it still continues unabated today!

All the natural resources of Tibet had been feverishly extracted and ferried to China without any thought to the disturbance of the ecological balance and economic condition of Tibet. I heard that there is a mountain behind Gyangste Palkhor Temple. A mother and son visited that mountain one day and found a diamond. They did not know what it was and asked a Chinese. The Chinese took it away from them, and the mother and son were provided with a house to live in, and two hundred Chinese Renminbi each per month, as their wages. This is just one example of how the Chinese deceive Tibetan people. It is said that all the national debt of China is being paid by the mining of borax in Tibet.

The Chinese continue to send five-hundred truckloads of timber a day from Chamdo in eastern Tibet to China. The same thing is happening in the other areas of Tibet, where there was once an abundance of forest wealth. When the Chinese came to Tibet they had nothing to bring except their sleeping bags, mugs, and guns, but on their return they have truckloads and truckloads of goods to take back to their homeland China. Where do you think they got all this raw material?

* * *

I was released in January 1981 and returned home to Gojo. When I visited my birthplace, after my release from prison, only one or two of my acquaintances and relatives were alive. The rest of them had perished. Some of them had been killed, and some had died of starvation and suffering.

When I went home, I did not have even a place to stay. All our property, from the house, to a needle, had been confiscated during the so-called liberation. I had to stay there as a guest of one of the families. Actually I was supposed to be provided with some sort of sustenance after my release, but they did not give me anything. They had redistributed all the private lands of rich families to the general public, and all other moveable assets like gold and silver ornaments, furniture, images of the deities, and even pots and pans were carried off to China.

***

I had always hoped to see His Holiness the Dalai Lama. Now that I was out of prison, I contemplated on how to go about it. I immediately decided to leave for India. I came in the end of 1981 and met His Holiness. I had been intercepted in Dram (Zhangmu) and beaten very badly. I had only a hundred yuan. That was all I had [to cover] bus fare, food expenses, or any other necessity. I clutched my money tightly and decided to offer it to His Holiness. So, I walked. I did not dare board a bus. I begged for food as I walked.

We three, the ones who had escaped together, were intercepted by the Chinese in Dram at dawn. I did not have valuable possessions. My clothes were poor. It had not been long since I had been released from the prison. I was old. When I had gone to prison, I was about twenty-five years old. When I came out, I was an old woman. I had spent my life in prison.

The Chinese intercepted us and interrogated us thoroughly. They took notes, the names of our county and village. After doing this, we were asked to go back to where we came from. After crossing a path, we hired a guide. He guided us into Barabsi, Nepal. In Nepal, we went to the Reception Center. They helped us to go to India.

I stayed in Nepal for about a dozen days. Thereafter, the Reception Center guided me to Dharamsala. They paid my bus fares. I had only a hundred yuan. Then, I had an audience with His Holiness. I offered fifty yuan to His Holiness and kept the remaining amount for myself.

* * *

Then, I went back. It occurred to me that it was not good if I would die without having done any useful work either of religious or of political nature, so I decided to leave my village for Lhasa. In Lhasa I persistently worked hard for the cause of Tibetan independence. I spent a month in Lhasa and made for my village. I spoke to the people in my village and motivated them. I told them that now we should not tolerate it any longer, and that we should fight for the independence of Tibet.

I motivated the people and spent about three months in my village. Then I went to Lhasa. In Lhasa we communicated to each other, we networked with all the important people we knew, and had discussions. We decided that we could not stay idle now that His Holiness was working hard in foreign countries and that now we must also try to rise up. For some years, we met and had discussions like this. Finally, we managed to rise up on September 27, 1987.

The monks of Drepung or Sera led the demonstration. The people followed them. There were large crowds of people. A police station was torched. We then marched towards the AR government office. As we reached Dhaley Thang, from where the fate of the AR government office could be seen, the Chinese police came and arrested the demonstrators. Thereafter, there were several demonstrations. I participated in all except for some organized by nuns.

Two Chinese spies kept an eye on me. They wanted to find out what I was doing, with whom I was staying, with whom I was having contacts, etc. I was to be arrested a couple days ago. I felt that no one had seen me. But I got a word from the PSB office that there were two people watching me. I was warned to be on my guard.

I had to go underground for over a year. Finally, I could not hide any longer and was forced to come to India. If I had stayed there, our organization would have suffered.

* * *

I have heard that these days, that the Chinese use various unbelievable methods to punish the prisoners in Tibet. They extract blood from the bodies of prisoners and use it for the purpose of blood transfusion in their own hospitals. We get this information from some of the nuns of Shugsep Nunnery, who escaped from Tibet very recently.

I have told you a brief story about myself. There are people who suffered much worse than me and there are people who suffered like me. In the whole of Tibet, there is not even a palm-sized land on which people have not suffered like this. To talk about monasteries, the lamas, the Tulkus, the abbots, the storekeepers, the disciplinarians and chant leaders, one is jailed. This is what really happened in our village. People under them were jailed, subjected to struggle sessions. Human feces were stuffed into the mouths while people were made to watch. They were beaten and asked many questions. Many people died under the violence of struggle sessions.

I am still ready to sacrifice my life for the cause of Tibet. If time and circumstances warrant that by giving away my life it is going to benefit the cause of liberating Tibet, and help fulfill the wishes of His Holiness, I am ready to give my life without a second thought.

TANAG JIGME SANGPO

Tanag Jigme Sangpo, age 64, was born in Chusar (near Lhasa). He is currently a prisoner at Lhasa Drapchi Prison (TAR Prison No. 1), serving a twenty-eight year term, after two increased terms of five and eight years. Since 1964 he has spent all his life in Chinese prisons and labor camps in Tibet, and is sentenced until September 2, 2011. He is one of the most prominent prisoners of conscience and one of the longest imprisoned Tibetan political prisoners in Chinese-occupied Tibet.

TANAG JIGME SANAG was arrested for the first time in 1964, while the Panchen Lama was being subjected to public beatings and humiliation during a torture-interrogation session known as *thamzing*. He was arrested for his 70,000-character petition submitted to the then Chinese Premiere Chao Enlai on May 18, 1962 which outlined in detail the suffering of the Tibetan people under Chinese rule.

According to Ven. Palden Gyatso (a 63 year-old monk who spent thirty-three years in Chinese prisons and labor camps and was closely associated with Tanag in his non-violent struggle for Tibetan freedom), Tanag was unable to endure it any more and blurted out with enthusiasm: "The Chinese seat themselves on our head and then talk down to us. This shouldn't be!" Tanag was a teacher at Zishing Lodra, the first Chinese-established school in Lhasa. During a meeting of the entire school, a fellow teacher informed the Chinese authorities of his reactionary behavior, and he was bitterly condemned. Tanag was dispactched to Yi Zhi Dui (as it was then known) re-education through labor unit of Sangyip Prison, Lhasa, to serve a term of three years. He completed his term in 1967.

As is customary of the Chinese justice administration system, he was not released at this time, but was put to work as a hired worker at a work brigade (Tibetan: *lemi rukhag*; Chinese: *zhigong*). He remained under surveillance and was subjected to a strictly regimented life.

Tanag had never been married. He had a sister who died young and left her son and two daughters. His niece was twenty-one years old at the time and had become a member of an underground Tibetan youth organization dedicated to Tibetan independence. The organization was formed and active during the chaotic years of the Cultural Revolution in China. The Chinese uncovered the organization with the arrest of some of its members. Tanag's niece fled Lhasa out of fear of arrest with the intention to escape from Tibet. When she reached Dhingri, southeast of Lhasa, the Chinese caught her and a photo of her uncle, which she was carrying, was found. Tanag was immediately arrested under suspicion of his involvement in the underground youth organization. For an entire year he was kept in chains, tortured, interrogated, and was brought for *thamzing* at all public meetings. His niece committed suicide in prison out of fear of execution. In 1970, nine members of the youth organization were executed at an enforced public meeting in Lhasa Powl Lingka.

Tanag was sentenced to a ten-year imprisonment term in 1970 for counter-revolutionary crimes. After completing his term, he was again retained as a hired or retained worker at the brick and clay-slate production unit no. 1—a work brigade at Nyethang. While at this work brigade there were successive arrests from the brigades of Ven. Lobsang Wangchuk (a monk-scholar who was one of Tibet most well-known political prisoners before his death in prison by torture), and Ven. Palden Gyatso. Both were active with him in continuing poster campaigns calling for Tibet's independence.

Tanag became very agitated at these arrests. Consequently, on July 15, 1983, he hung a large wall poster at Lhasa Barkhor and circumambulated Tibet's holiest shrine, the Jokhang, with a white banner around his body, as he triumphantly sang the Tibetan national anthem. After about ten days, the PSB searched his home and found five different reactionary propaganda materials. He was again arrested and put in Gutsa Prison, Lhasa. On November 24, 1983, he was sentenced to a fifteen-year imprisonment term and put in Drapchi Prison.

While in Drapchi he was informed about the demonstrations on September 27, 1987 by Drepung monks, and reacted by shouting and raising slogans on October 5, 1987, congratulating the monks and calling on his fellow prisoners to join the freedom fighters. He ran through the aisles of the prison cafeteria with a poster that read: "The Communist Chinese Occupational Army Should Go Back!" He was tried for spreading and inciting counter-revolutionary propaganda and sentenced to an additional term of five years in jail, bringing his compounded prison term to twenty years.

On December 6, 1991, a Swiss human rights delegation visited Drapchi Prison. The prisoners realized that important foreign dignitaries were visiting when political prisoners were hidden in a remote section of the prison behind the re-education through labor apple orchard, and by pork (which was served to the prisoners), only to be taken back as soon as the visitors left. The visitors were shown how wonderfully the prisoners were being fed, and were presented ordinary criminals dressed as counter-revolutionary elements who having taken part in demonstrations were now actively undergoing reform, etc.

Tanag had a reputation for raising slogans for foreign

visitors. On this occasion he was separated from the other political prisoners and detained under close surveillance in the room where prison cooks and their bedrooms. When the foreign visitors arrived, he immediately raised slogans, thwarting the attempt of the prison guards who tried to gag him. He shouted in broken English, Tibetan and Chinese: "Long live His Holiness, The Dalai Lama. Long Live the Tibetan Nation" and demanded the visitors help Tibet regain its independence as it had the right to freedom under international law. When the visitors heard him they asked the Chinese authorities what he was shouting about. The Chinese authorities replied that it was a mad man shouting.

He was subjected to severe beatings and detained in solitary confinement for this behavior. A new method of which he experienced at the time was exposure to extremely cold temperature. Large sheets of metal were erected on all sides of his isolated cell in order to lower the ambient temperature of the already very cold cell. The average temperature in Lhasa (3,200 meters above sea level) at that time in January was about -3.2C dropping to -10C at times.

He was tried again and has now been sentenced to an additional term of eight years in prison. His total prison term now stands at twenty-eight years.

Since his arrest in 1964 Tanag Jigme Sangpo has known no free life. He has spent his entire life in Chinese prisons and labor camps. Appeals for help have been received from Tibet on his behalf; extra clothes and aid are not allowed to be sent to him. According to his former prison mate, Ven. Palden Gyatso, during his previous ten-year jail term he had become completely blind. He is now stated to be able to see slightly through one eye. There is no picture of him available.

Tanag was being trained as a civil servant in independent Tibet.

NGAWANG WANGDOL

Ngawant Wangdol, a nineteen-year-old nun from Lhokhar was sentenced to three years of imprisonment for expressing her thoughts aloud in the Barkhor in 1992.

I WAS BORN into a peasant family, with two younger brothers and two sisters, one younger and the other the eldest. I stayed at home and helped my mother with household chores.

At the age of thirteen I joined the Mehuri Monastery, where I studied for three years. Five nuns and a monk from Sera joined me in staging a cry against the oppression of the Chinese. On the 3rd of February 1992, we walked down to Lhasa and shouted slogans in praise of His Holiness the Dalai Lama. When we had almost completed a round, we were pulled back and thrown into a van where we were beaten. At the *Kuwathing* (Chinese office) we were interrogated and had to [give our] thumbprint[s]. We were then taken to Gutsa Prison, where we were thoroughly searched and kept in solitary confinement. We were made to stand upright against the wall and were beaten severely late into the night. The four nuns and monk were sent to Drapchi Prison after six months at Gutsa. My friend and I were minors and so were detained in Gutsa for one year and six months. Our case was not settled for one year because we were under age for a trial. We applied and pleaded for a quick trial, but we were sentenced to three years of imprisonment.

At Gutsa, we were made to remove feces and use them as manure in the vegetable gardens. The cells where we were confined were very dirty with urine and the ground was used as a toilet. The Chinese came several times to draw blood from the

Tibetan prisoners. Fortunately, I was sick the first time and out at work other times.

We were made to count the number of prisoners in our own cells in Chinese every morning. Once my friend burst out in laughter, while counting, upon which we were kept on the roof of the green house with no food. We were left there for many hours in the cold winter rain. A Tibetan boy tried to smuggle some tingmo forks, but he was seen and beaten, together with the use of electric current.

If while counting in Chinese a mistake was made, one would be severely punished.

We were given half-cooked food, which was usually dirty, soiled with mud or manure. Sometimes, generous garden keepers would give us some radishes. We were accused of stealing the radishes and had to stand in the hot sun (thirty of us) for four hours and were made to eat many stalks of radishes.

Many cried unable to eat more but were kicked and beaten. We all suffered from diarrhea and stomachache. We spent the next year and six months at Trison Prison. It was September 25th when we reached Trison. Here, there were very few prisoners and we had to work or move. Here too we had to remove feces and use it as manure on the vegetables, which we had to grow. Eleven prisoners had to earn 26,000 yuan in one year from the vegetables sold. If you could make more, the excess would be shared by the officers while we would be rewarded by better food on that day. We also had to cut rocks and plant bamboo.

On Losar, we managed to smuggle a cassette recorder through relatives who had come to meet some prisoners. We recorded songs of freedom, folk, and prayers for four days. A nun gave a visiting relative a cassette but this was confiscated. A series of interrogations followed, where the Chinese wanted to know the object of such recordings. We denied that it was meant to be sent across to India. We were told that our term would be prolonged as was done with the Drapchi prisoners who had sung freedom songs. This, however, was not done but the vigilance become strict and we were given more work and less leisure. Meeting visitors was not allowed for some time.

We then heard that a friend, Phintso Yangki, had passed away in the Drapchi prison. We planned a demonstration on the last of October, an important Chinese festival day. While collecting water, we threw it on the electrician, who complained about it. An officer questioned us. A woman (prison assistant) abused us, calling us prostitutes. There was commotion as we fought against her. Then we were rounded and told that we were to be sent to *Kanju, Thonga-dushi* (the dark cell). A woman guard allowed us to use the toilet, where we decided to stage the planned demonstration immediately. As we were pushed in to the dark cell, we shouted slogans against the Chinese. Thereupon we were dragged out into the compound, kicked by fifty or sixty soldiers. The cattle prod and rubber batons were used. We had to kneel down on the cemented floor. A nun put her shoes under the knees [and] for this she was severely punished.

Some fainted and fell unconscious. A nun fell and was dragged to the dark cell. Another nun was kept to keep vigil over her. We were then put away in the solitary dark cell at 3:30 a.m. Three nuns were taken back to their previous cells after three days. Five of us were kept for seven days, with no quilts. We spent many sleepless nights in the winter cold. We had to go without food on the first day. The next day we were fed *tingmo* and a cup of black tea. We were interrogated and beaten. The cattle prod was used inside our mouths, behind our ears and between the fingers. We were held back by the Chinese, who caught us by our hair, and were kicked. I was told to sign a paper where I would be held responsible for the actions of the five Mejuri nuns. I agreed on the conditions that two sick nuns be removed from the dark cell to their previous cells.

My knee hurt and my shirt was bloodied. I realized that my ear lobe had been torn and was bleeding. They cleaned up all the blood in case the other prisoners would see it.

I was sent back to the previous cell on the seventeenth of August 1994. We had to wash all the clothes of the army camp close to the prison in the winter-cold water. The police would be paid for the laundry. We had to attend talks given by the Chinese, for fourteen days, where we were told good things about the Chinese, the development in Tibet and the condemnation of His Holiness the Dalai Lama. We then had to write all that was told in the meetings and submit it the next day. We were shown movies in which demonstrators were punished in other foreign countries. Every Saturday, we had to learn Chinese songs in praise of Mao Zedong. We were beaten if we could not sing on our own. The men especially were tortured if they failed to learn the songs. During the winter months, we had to undergo rigorous military training, and were uselessly beaten and abused. We were warned against telling visitors about such beatings. We were told to tell visitors that this was not a prison but a re-education school.

After our persistent complaints, a Tibetan official was sent to supervise the training.

I was released on the 2nd of February 1995. I went home. My father had passed away while I was in prison. After two months, I came to Lhasa and met prisoner friends at Trison and saw friends at Drapchi. In the meantime, my friend Sherab Ngawang, from Meta-gongka, had succumbed to her injuries on the 17th of February in 1995. While in prison, the excessive beatings had destroyed her kidneys and stomach.

Realizing the futility of living in Chinese-occupied Lhasa, I left with friends on the 26th of September 1995. We reached Dharamsala on the 22nd of October 1995.

APHO GHAKA, A.K.A. PHAGCHUK GONPO

Apho Ghaka is 55 years old. He was born in 1943 at Bher Chamdo. He presently works in the security office of the Tibetan Government-in-Exile in Dharamsala.

I WAS ARRESTED in November 1960 in the course of a fight with Chinese occupational forces at Lhathog Ganyag under Chamdo district and subsequently was detained for nineteen years. I was first imprisoned in Chamdo monastery, which was converted into a prison for one year. Later I was transferred to Sithog prison (the biggest prison in all the thirteen districts under Chamdo) for six years. In 1963, I was sentenced to life imprisonment and transferred to the Second AR prison in Powo in Chamdo district where I was detained for the next ten years. From the time of my arrest until 1969, when I was detained at Powo, my feet where chained. In March 1976 I was transferred to Lhasa and was put in Drapchi prison. In March 1979 I was released along with a small group of Tibetans (most of whom had been in prison since 1959).

* * *

Before I was sentenced I was not forced to labor. But after being sentenced I was forced to wash the laundry of the prison officials and guards. When I was transferred to Powo prison I was forced to do carpentry. In our prison the prisoners made wooden window and door frames, shelves, chairs and tables, frames for the roofs, and boxes. There were thirty to forty prisoners who did carpentry for at least ten hours every day. The

115

prison office had to account for all the wood products made by the prisoners. These products were sold to other Chinese offices and transported to China. A chair would be sold for thirty yuan and a table for sixty yuan. No money was given to the prisoners. We were given three meals daily. On Sunday, which was usually a holiday, there were only two meals. They usually consisted of tsampa (not made from barley but from wheat) and steamed bread.

In the other seven prisons belonging to Powo prison, prisoners were forced to work in the fields, to cut down forests, construct roads and buildings, work in the poultry farms and pig-sties, look after the apple, orange and walnut orchards, build bridges and work as blacksmiths. Prisoners were also forced to do tailoring in these eight prisons, especially in Zongna prison. The prisons would make shirts and pants (including Mao suits) for the market, night suits and hats, quilt covers, pillow cases, jackets, and socks. The finished products were mostly sold to private businessmen and wholesale retailers. During *Zakhor Kunjud* (*Sing Ho Qen Dog in Chinese*), a weekly meeting of prisoners, the prison officials punished prisoners who were unable to produce the required number of items. These prisoners sometimes had their prison terms extended, were forced to work more hours, had their food ration reduced, and were sometimes even executed.

There was also an annual meeting known in Chinese as *Tong Shue* (in Chinese it means inter re-education.) In these meetings, prisoners who defended the religion or independence of Tibet, or uttered mantras or statements favoring Tibetan independence, were punished through *thamzings* or struggle sessions in front of all the prisoners. Some prisoners whose yearly record had not been favorable in the eyes of the prison authorities would face *thamzing* or other forms of torture such as being chained or tied from the ceiling.

The other six prisons in Powo are:

1. Dongchu Prison (where I was detained for ten years after being sentenced to life imprisonment in 1963). Most prisoners, almost a thousand, would work in the fields and others would work as black smiths, carpenters, or tailors.

2. Chumdho Prison (formerly Chamdo monastery which was converted into a prison in 1959). Most of the 800 prisoners here worked in the fields and a small number worked as blacksmiths and tailors.

3. Nadhep Prison had around 400 to 500 prisoners. Most of the prisoners worked in the fields or in deforesting units. The whole region of Powo (Southwest Kham, bordering Kongpo in U-tsang) was very rich in forest resources, which included pinewood, walnut wood, *wose* (Tibetan), sandalwood, and *latra* (Tibetan). Most of the wood was transported from Tramo (in the same region) to China.

4. Tramo Prison had over 1,000 prisoners, most of whom were involved with lumbering and constructing Chinese military installations and offices.

5. Tralung Prison contained from 300 to 500 prisoners, most of whom had to work in the agricultural fields or orchards, as well as take care of the pigs and chickens.

6. Gushang Prison detained from 300 to 500 prisoners, most of whom had to make bricks.

During my ten years of imprisonment in various prisons in Powo region I mainly made wooden boxes, approximately one hundred a year. These boxes were sold in the market for 60 Yuan each in Lhasa. Most of the products were transported to

China. There were times when I was forced to work over four hours during the night.

In 1976, I was transferred to Drapchi prison in Lhasa and was detained in the cells of the second unit, again assigned to work in the carpentry section. I worked in this section until my release in 1979. There were around 1,000 prisoners in Drapchi prison during that period. Over 200 prisoners worked in the tailoring section and made shirts, pants, socks, quilt and pillow covers, jackets, coats, and hats. Around 100 prisoners would do the stitching part alone. Between 300 and 400 prisoners were assigned to stone breaking or shaping. Many prisoners were assigned to look after the vegetable gardens. The vegetables would be sold in the Lhasa market. Prisoners were also forced to make cement containers and sacks to be used by the cement factories. At least thirty trucks would transport these items to the factories. Prisoners also did construction work, blacksmith, and garage work where they repaired vehicles. At Drapchi Prison, prisoners were made to work from eight to nine hours a day.

After my release I was sent to Tsethang, the headquarters of eight districts. In the *Lhemi Rughak* (work unit) I had to do construction work and carpentry. There were around 300 Tibetans in this work unit and we were paid 44 Yuan per month for working eight to nine hours every day.

I am now fifty-five years old and live in Dharamsala as a Tibetan refugee.

Tibetans of Utah

An article by Billy Jackson

In saffron and maroon robes, the Dalai Lama stands by a still mountain lake that reflects the thousand-roomed Potala Palace. His expression does not betray the tragedy being suffered by the people he was forced to leave. Slapped across the picture, a bright yellow banner reads, THE ESCAPE THAT ROCKED THE REDS.

This painted scene adorned the cover of Time magazine's 20 April, 1959 edition, which sold for 25 cents and recounted the escape of Tibet's most eminent exile.

In October 1950, the Chinese "liberated" and occupied Tibet. China's human rights record in the country ever since has been among the worst of the century.

Since the Dalai Lama's flight into India over forty years ago, hundreds of thousands of Tibetans have slipped past trigger-happy border guards and braved the highest mountain passes in the world to flee a country they say is controlled through fear. Thousands perished in the attempt, but those who survived are scattered across the globe, from New Delhi to Zurich—and even to Salt Lake City.

In fact, Utah is home to a veritable community of refugee Tibetans that is almost 200 strong. Thanks in part to the Utah Tibetan Resettlement Project, a program set up by some of the first exiles to reach the area in the late 1980s, scores of political outcasts have made their way to the Beehive State.

But the exiles aren't the only Tibetans in Utah. A small group of students are here as part of exchange programs between China and state colleges. And though they are

119

benefiting from an American education thanks to their new masters in Beijing, even these Tibetans harbor a deep-felt resentment for the Chinese government presence in their homeland.

"Nobody wants the Chinese in Tibet," said one Utah Valley State College student from Lhasa who wishes to remain anonymous. "They destroy our culture and don't let us venerate His Holinesss the Dalai Lama."

But while these students are here by choice, others are here because they can't go home.

Tenzin Norbu only knows the season he was born in, but guesses that he is about fifty-four years old. He is from Kham, the southeastern part of Tibet known for its warrior-like people called Khampas. He has thick black hair and a rugged face to match the harsh stories he tells of life in Tibet.

As a young boy, he watched on as his uncle was shot by Chinese troops. The rest of his family was compelled to scatter for their own safety, and Tenzin decided to join the resistance guerillas to fight a losing battle against superior technology and far superior numbers. When most of the fighters had been killed or had retreated to the safety of India or Nepal, Tenzin kept on fighting.

It wasn't until he killed a high-ranking Chinese officer that Tenzin was caught.

Thrown into prison and forced to wear all black, the exile remembers hours-long, daily political education and signs on the walls that read, "Don't Follow the Dalai Lama." There were sixteen major rules in the prison, but Tenzin was most angered by rule number one: no prayers.

"My first punishment [for breaking the rules] was getting my face stuck in a container of gunpowder, then having it lit," Norbu said. "It burned my face and hair."

Once, upon refusal to clean up prisoners excrement with his bare hands, Tenzin Norbu was force-fed the feces on the end of a shovel by prison guards.

"There was a lot done in the prison that you can't imagine," Norbu said.

According to Tenzin, the Chinese would experiment various torture devices on the Tibetan prisoners. Once, he was forced to wear self-tightening handcuffs until his whole body went numb.

"I saw lights, like stars were flashing," Norbu said.

After passing out, Tenzin came to—to the amazement of his fellow prisoners. Tenzin remembers them saying, "You have awoken from your death!"

By this time, the Khampa had spent more than eight years in prison. Then one night the guards told him that he had less than two years left—then he would be executed.

That was the night Tenzin Norbu resolved to escape.

After feigning sickness, he and a fellow inmate were taken to the prison hospital where he underwent actual surgery despite his healthy condition. That night, they were able to escape past drunk sentries.

In 1984, an exhausted Tenzin stumbled into a Tibetan refugee camp in Nepal, having *walked* all the way from Lhasa (over six hundred miles) nursing a stomach torn up during an unnecessary operation.

After trying his lot in Nepal, India, and Boston, Tenzin Norbu settled in Salt Lake City. But life in America wasn't especially easy, either.

"I didn't know English," he said. "My wife was sick. I didn't know what insurance was. I didn't know what I was supposed to do with hospital bills."

But he learned, and though he still works menial jobs as a

janitor and a dishwasher, he values the freedom he enjoys here.

"Everyone [in Utah] has his or her freedom," he said. "It's the only thing that keeps me somewhat happy."

For the most part, the Khampa just misses home.

But Tenzin Norbu is only one of several Tibetan refugees in Utah to have spent time in Chinese prisons.

Tashi Paldon is fifty-eight years old but looks like she's ninety. Her scraggly gray hair is tied up in a bun, and her dress is the traditional Tibetan style.

"Since the Chinese occupation," she said through an interpreter, "Tibetans did not want to stay under Chinese rule."

That was why Paldon's older brother decided to leave Tibet for India to be with the Dalai Lama, and why Paldon encouraged him to go. She helped pack his bag.

And for that vile act of disloyalty to the state she was locked up for fifteen years.

Her experiences in prison match Tenzin Norbu's.

"Prisoners would fight over mice and leftovers," Paldon said. "Sometimes they would eat human feces. It was said that Chinese excrement was worse than Tibetan excrement."

Among other things, Paldon remembers eating human flesh dropped by vultures from Tibetan funerals; manual labor carrying rocks that the men had broken; international studies that began by condemning America and India and concluded with a forced, signed personal essay attacking the two countries; no visits, ever; and routine executions.

"There was a meeting," Paldon said. "They called all the prisoners together. We weren't allowed to look around or even look at each other. Whenever these meetings were called, we knew that someone would die. Though we did not witness the execution, someone was always missing when we returned to our cells."

Torture was common, and every morning Paldon would wake to the screams of the male prisoners on the other side of the wall.

In spite of these conditions, the outside world has chosen to remain strangely ignorant of it all, though this lack of knowledge is due in part to Chinese methods of concealment, says Paldon.

"Whenever foreigners visited, the guards made us change our clothes and made sure we were clean. They tidied up the prison and changed everything, including the bed mattresses."

Paldon said that people often tried to commit suicide but couldn't. Electric shocks and cattle prods were used as punishment devices. The woman burst into tears when she told the story of her friend, a fellow prisoner, who was executed for tearing down a poster.

But even in the face of her prison experience, Paldon says that her most painful memory did not occur behind bars.

"The hardest day of my life was when my brother was executed by the Chinese," Paldon said. "I was there. I remember the faces of my brother and his friends were unrecognizable because they were beaten so badly. Something was put in their mouths to prevent them from praising His Holiness [the Dalai Lama]."

Except for one, the twelve boys executed that day were all between the ages of thirteen and nineteen.

"Our families were forced to thank the officials for executing our sons and brothers," she said.

And now Paldon lives in Utah, unable to speak English and afraid to leave the house for fear of embarrassment.

She spends most of her time praying. An air of hopelessness pervades her cramped apartment.

Scores of Tibetans, however, have made a smoother

transition into American society, especially those born and raised in exile. Tibetan children in Salt Lake City, for example, wear name brand clothes and speak English with a Utah accent. Their friends are all American and they look forward to attending American universities.

When representatives of the Karmapa, the third-highest position in the Tibetan religious hierarchy, visited Salt Lake City in 1999, they noted that the mountains of the Wasatch Front (the Rocky Mountains that line the east side of the Salt Lake valley) reminded them of Tibet. Perhaps it is the snow-capped peaks that draw Tibetans to Utah.

Such a conclusion would agree with the penned words of the late Ngodup Paljor, a refugee Tibetan who found refuge in another American wilderness:

> Some come to Alaska
> To dig the frozen tundra
> And others to hibernate
> In igloos
> Well, comrades, to tell
> You my reason,
> Where else could a yak live,
> Besides in wilderness and
> Mountain

Unfortunately, for some only the mountains of Tibet can bring solace.

Official Statement:

Department of Health, Tibetan Government-In-Exile

TIBETAN TORTURE SURVIVORS PROGRAM

Those of us who enjoy peace and freedom without having had to suffer for them, have the moral duty to ensure that the persecuted, the wounded, and the tortured, receive care, gratitude, and the possibility of recovering their human potential. —Dr. Oscar A. Sanchez

IN THE WAKE of the Chinese occupation of Tibet in 1959, His Holiness the Dalai Lama, the spiritual and temporal leader of Tibet, and about 85,000 Tibetan followers, escaped from Tibet and sought refuge or political asylum in India. A long silence prevailed until 1979, which, for the first time, saw a little more relaxed policy of the Chinese with the opening doors for the Tibetans, in and outside Tibet, to meet each other. Later, with the strengthening of the Chinese policy in 1987-88, massive political uprisings erupted in Tibet. The Tibetan people took to the streets of Lhasa, the capital city of Tibet, to voice against the hegemonic Chinese regime, only to be crushed mercilessly. This program was initiated in response to the escalating tyrannical and oppressive policies of the occupying Chinese, leading to influx of a large number of newly arrived Tibetans into India, while negotiating the tiresome journey across the rugged Himalayas. Many of them suffered from physical and psychological torture under the oppressive Chinese rule. While not all of them require medical treatment, a sufficient number of them need special counseling, medical support, and treatment to adapt to the new environment.

The Tibetan Torture Survivors Program—a special component under the Department of Health, Central Tibetan Administration—was started in the early 1990's, but was launched as a full-fledged program with proper staffing only in October 1996...

The initial few years, between 1990 and 1996, were spent on procuring funds and general skill development by establishing contacts with numerous donor groups, mental health experts, and adept medical professionals in drawing up a mutually cohesive diagnostic skills treatment and rehabilitation plan. Parallel to this, several joint pilot studies were carried out to assess the extent/impact of physical and psychological torture inflicted upon them, needs assessment of these people, and towards developing a comprehensive rehabilitation, treatment, and management of trauma program.

TTSP is headed by a Program Officer who holds the managerial task to oversee the proper functioning of the program. It is a multi-disciplinary forum comprising a team of Tibetan traditional doctors, spiritual advisors/consultants, allopathic doctors, expatriate psychologists, and doctors and social workers to cater to the psycho/social and mental health care needs of clients through a collective, integrated system of both the Tibetan traditional medicine and modern allopathic medicine, aimed towards this end. The program undertakes the overall responsibility of looking after the Tibetan victims of torture who have endured severe forms of traumatization, and it seeks to reduce physical, psychosocial, and psychological sequel resulting from organized violence and politically motivated torture in Tibet.

Treatment

TTSP provides cost-free medical and psychological assistance to Tibetan victims of torture and other forms of political repression. The mode of treatment is both Tibetan traditional medicine and allopathic medicine, depending upon the choice of the clients. Individual counseling therapy, psycho-therapy, or supportive therapy and regular monthly group therapy sessions are also accorded to the needful, with greater emphasis on *lojong* or raining of mind to develop a practical coping mechanism against any stressful circumstances. The cases which can not be handled here...are referred to bigger Indian hospitals, after a prior recommendation by the doctor concerned. All medical expenses, including traveling and daily allowances, are borne by the program along with expenses for the interpreter and the helper.

Rehabilitation

One of the underlying objects of this program is to resettle and rehabilitate these people in a new socio-cultural environment. In the process of rehabilitation, the clients are offered services/assistance such as social support in the form of monthly allowances, stipends, housing allowances, and rehabilitation of torture survivors who are too old to work, as well as vocational or livelihood training seeking to make them capable of self-support and self-reliance after a few years of help.

Printed in the United Kingdom
by Lightning Source UK Ltd.
117891UK00001BB/41